THE UNIVERSITY OF CHICAGO

ENVIRONMENTAL

PERCEPTION

AND BEHAVIOR

DEPARTMENT OF GEOGRAPHY
RESEARCH PAPER NO. 109

David Lowenthal, editor
American Geographical Society

Chicago • Illinois
1967

Second printing, April 1968
Third printing, September 1969

155.9
En 89

Research Papers
1101 E. 58th Street
Chicago, Illinois 60637

Library of Congress Catalog Card Number: 66-29233

A Note on the Text and the Contributors

The papers in this volume are edited versions of those presented in a symposium of the same title at the sixty-first annual meeting of the Association of American Geographers, Columbus, Ohio, April 20, 1965. The inspiration and organization of the symposium were the work of Robert W. Kates. At the Columbus symposium, Gilbert F. White of the University of Chicago served as chairman, and presented an introductory framework, and David Lowenthal offered a concluding summary and commentary. The substantive papers were read in the order in which they appear in the text.

> Robert Beck is Post-Doctoral Fellow in Psychology, New York University, and Consultant in Behavioral Science, Regional Plan Association, New York.

> Robert W. Kates is Associate Professor of Geography, Clark University.

> David Lowenthal is Research Associate, American Geographical Society, New York.

> Kevin Lynch is Associate Professor of City Planning, Massachusetts Institute of Technology; Donald Appleyard is Assistant Professor of Urban Design, and John Myer is Assistant Professor of Architecture at the same institution.

> Joseph Sonnenfeld is Associate Professor of Geography, University of Delaware.

> Yi-Fu Tuan is Associate Professor of Geography, University of Toronto.

TABLE OF CONTENTS

LIST OF TABLES

LIST OF ILLUSTRATIONS

INTRODUCTION: ENVIRONMENTAL PERCEPTION AND BEHAVIOR

David Lowenthal

The universe of geographical study may be divided into three realms: the nature of the environment; what we think and feel about the environment; and how we behave in, and alter, that environment. These realms are everywhere interrelated. None can be understood in isolation, but each of the three requires such different techniques of analysis, that they are, in fact, usually studied by separate disciplines.

Until recently, geographers have mainly been content to explore the first of these realms -- that is, what they consider the real world. Yet in daily practise, we all subordinate reality to the world we perceive, experience, and act in. We respond to and affect the environment not directly, but through the medium of a personally apprehended milieu. This milieu differs for each of us according to his personal history; and for each of us it varies also with mood, with purpose, and with attentiveness. What we see, what we study, and the way we shape and build in the landscape is selected and structured for each of us by custom, culture, desire, and faith. To understand perceptual processes requires examination of all these facets of human behavior.

It is with such processes that the papers in this book are principally concerned -- processes that illumine environmental perception and behavior. Thought and feeling are essential clues to understanding the interactions of man and milieu. These papers demonstrate that subjective, often unconscious, and culturally dominated forces play a major role in how we see the environment and act in it; and that scientific interpretations of the universe are only partial models of the more complex structures that individuals sense and interpret.

The authors here represented go beyond geography's traditional forays into mathematics, economics, geology, and astrophysics to enter the equally difficult but fruitful fields of metaphysics, behavioral psychology, the history of ideas, social

1

anthropology, and architecture. At the same time, they are uncommonly earthbound, tied to concrete things that can be seen, heard, smelled, or visualized -- mountains, directions, potatoes, Gardens of Eden, road surfaces, deserts, running streams, fruits. The objects these images relate to are not all real or extant, but they stand for specific sense data, the bedrock, so to speak, of geographical experience.

The range of research herein described is as broad as the subject of perception is comprehensive. By scrutinizing literary, artistic, and ethnographic data from the perspectives of culture history, and the history of ideas, Yi-Fu Tuan shows how writers and painters have seen and reacted to different types of landscape. Robert Beck, Joseph Sonnenfeld, and Kevin Lynch seek to ascertain how people feel about various aspects of their milieus, Beck for isolated elementary properties of space, Sonnenfeld for physical environments as wholes, and Lynch for landscape features seen in sequence by commuters. Robert Kates goes beyond matters of taste and preference to predictions about behavior -- what environmental conditions do people anticipate, and how would they respond to expected hazards? And he compares their responses with their actual behavior during crises.

The conclusions presented are significant in themselves. When considered together, they raise a host of new questions. What are the connections between responses to abstract spatial patterns and to gross environmental complexes? Can the extreme parameters of perception studied by Beck and by Sonnenfeld be amalgamated? How much bearing have expressions of preference on actual behavior patterns? Is group action in the environment simply the net sum of individual choices and decisions, or something more or less than this? We need to identify and study the range of response to key symbolic landscapes -- landscapes that perennially catch the attention of mankind and that seem to stand for, reflect, or incorporate, the meaning and purpose of life itself. Deserts and gardens, as Yi-Fu Tuan shows, carry some of this freighted significance; wilderness is another such locale. Topographic metaphors for personal and social experience have been shown to permeate the language and to dominate the behavior of some primitive tribes; we should seek for analogies to these in our own culture and society.

In studying native cosmologies for clues to environmental attitudes, as Tuan suggests, let us not neglect the post-Columbian natives of America. Underlying all our expressed attitudes toward the milieu is a core of assumptions and values about the nature of man and of nature. To cite two instances, our sense of the over-riding importance of the future can be shown to lead to a neglect of amenities in the present-day landscape and simultaneously to a self-conscious veneration of the scenic and historical heritage. And our tendency toward dialectics, toward viewing life in terms of one of just two alternatives, leads to the zoning of landscape as we compartmenta-lize life, in terms of man or nature, city or country, work or play.

These papers may stimulate some geographers to explore perceptual problems in greater depth. But the problems will not be neglected in any case, for they have practical as well as theoretical implications. Without a prior understanding of the bases of perception and behavior, environmental planning and improvement are mere academic exercises, doomed to failure because unrelated to the terms in which people think and the goals they select. Current concern for environmental quality has already led architects and psychologists, engineers and planners, to new ways of examining how man sees the earth he lives in, and how vision affects action. Such studies as these, moreover, stimulate awareness of habitat generally. And thereby they encourage the public to demand and, ultimately, to help create better environments everywhere.

CHAPTER I

ATTITUDES TOWARD ENVIRONMENT: THEMES AND APPROACHES

Yi-Fu Tuan

The hub of geographical concern is often signaled by a pair of terms like "man and land," "land and life," "man and environment." These flexible expressions, however, also label the interests of workers in other fields; not only the ecologist and the anthropologist, but the philosopher and the theologian write on themes that can be surveyed under such titles as "man and land" or "man and nature." For members of the geographical guild, the core area seems to lie in the spatial, mappable manifestations of the "man-land" synergism.

From this core, wayward spirits have, on occasion, diverged along two paths. One is well trodden; its signposts, as one moves away from the core area, may successively read: landforms, processes affecting landforms, the physics of the processes that affect landforms. The other path is perhaps less well marked. It leads from the material imprints man has left on nature to the agent, man (a force expressible in part by such quantitative data as population density), and then to the vector of that force, expressed in man's attitude toward nature. Movement from the core area thus leads in one direction to the physical sciences, and in the other -- by way of the social sciences -- to the humanities.

It is this humanistic fringe of our catholic field, the study of man's attitude toward his environment, that is considered here. First I shall survey some of the avenues that have already been followed -- an enumeration that serves to emphasize the diversity of possible humanistic approaches. Then I shall sketch a particular approach, one that, so far as I know, has not yet been much explored.

I

Studies of man's attitude toward nature are of varying thematic complexity. The approaches listed hereafter range roughly from simple to complex:

4

(1) <u>An individual's attitude toward a particular aspect of environment</u>. Scholars have, for example, scrutinized Constable's ideas and feelings about clouds,[1] and Thoreau's about weather.[2]

(2) <u>An individual's attitude toward a region</u>. Typical examples of this genre are "Wessex", as seen through the eyes of Thomas Hardy,[3] and the American West as perceived by John Muir.[4] Geographers so far have largely overlooked the work of novelists; the response of D. H. Lawrence to the English Midlands,[5] and of Willa Cather to the American Middle West,[6] to cite two instances, offer valuable insights. And it may be worthwhile to examine the personal responses of geographers as well: Vidal de la Blache's writings on France are worthy of review not only for their aperçu of France, but also for what they reveal of his own attitudes (in the philosophical context of the time), toward man and nature.

(3) <u>An individual's conception of the man-nature synergism</u>. This is the approach of the historian of ideas. Conceptions studied may be explicit and formalized, as in the works of natural philosophers and theologians, or implicit, as in the works of nature-poets. The views of such natural philosophers as Count Buffon and George Perkins Marsh have received scholarly attention.[7] Nor has the testimony of the nature-

[1] Kurt Badt, <u>John Constable's Clouds</u> trans. Stanley Godman, (London: Rutledge and Kegan Paul, 1950); L.C.W. Bonacina, "John Constable's Centenary: His Position as a Painter of Weather," <u>Quarterly Journal of the Royal Meteorological Society</u>, LXIII (1937), pp. 483-90.

[2] Lawrence Willson, "Thoreau and New England's Weather," <u>Weatherwise</u>, XII (1959), pp. 91-94.

[3] H.C. Darby, "The Regional Geography of Thomas Hardy's Wessex," <u>Geographical Review</u>, XXXVIII (1948), pp. 426-43.

[4] John Leighly, "John Muir's Image of the West," <u>Annals of the Association of American Geographers</u>, XLVIII (1948), pp. 309-18.

[5] D.H. Lawrence, "Nottingham and the Mining Country" (1929), in <u>Selected Essays</u> (Harmondsworth, Middlesex: Penguin Books, 1954), pp. 114-22.

[6] Willa Cather, <u>My Antonia</u> (Boston: Houghton Mifflin Co., 1918).

[7] Clarence J. Glacken, "Count Buffon on Cultural Changes of the Physical Environment," <u>Annals of the Association of American Geographers</u>, L (1960), pp. 1-21; David Lowenthal, <u>George Perkins Marsh: Versatile Vermonter</u> (New York: Columbia University Press, 1958).

poets been neglected.[8]

(4) The attitude of a people (or peoples) toward environment. Response to environment is most clearly formulated when a people, migrating from one country to another, leaves impressions of the new scene in writing. The United States, a land of recent immigrants, clearly yields many opportunities for this type of study, and the opportunities have not been neglected. The geographical literature on attitudes of Anglo-American settlers toward the Atlantic seaboard, and on their responses later, to such unfamiliar natural scenes as the prairies and the Great Plains, is slim, but significant.[9] South Africa and Australia, seen through the eyes of immigrants, may provide pertinent comparisons with the American experience. For the American Southwest, we can further compare responses to the same region by peoples of different cultural and climatic backgrounds. The evaluation of New Mexico by Latin American visitors, such as Bishop Tamarón and Antonio Barreiro, contrasted sharply with that of Anglo-Americans like Lieutenants J.H. Simpson and J.R. Bartlett.

A defect of this approach is its heavy dependence on literary evidence; undue weight may be given to the (perhaps wayward) opinions of the articulate few. Other types of evidence, however, may be used wherever available. They range from the

---

[8]Apart from the distinguished example of Alexander von Humboldt (Cosmos, a Sketch of a Physical Description of the Universe, II, 1870) among natural philosophers, there is an extensive literature on attitudes toward nature as revealed in poetical works. A small sample might include: John C. Shairp, On the Poetic Interpretation of Nature (Boston: Houghton, Mifflin and Company, 1890); A. Biese, The Development of the Feeling for Nature in the Middle Ages and Modern Times (New York: E. P. Dutton and Company, 1905); M. Blatt, The Treatment of Nature in German Literature from Gunther to the Appearance of Goethe's Werther (Chicago: 1902); Myra Reynolds, The Treatment of Nature in English Poetry between Pope and Wordsworth (2nd ed. Chicago: University of Chicago Press, 1909); Cornelius E. De Haas, Nature and the Country in English Poetry of the First Half of the Eighteenth Century (Amsterdam: H. J. Paris, 1928); Robert A. Aubin, Topographical Poetry in 18th Century England (New York, The Modern Language Association of America, 1936); Joseph W. Beach, Concept of Nature in 19th Century English Poetry (New York: MacMillan Company, 1936).

Books of a philosophical bent that see nature poetry as revelatory of nature include A. N. Whitehead's Science and the Modern World (New York: Mentor, 1948); Philip Wheelwright's The Burning Fountain (Bloomington: Indiana University Press, 1954) and N. P. Stallknecht's Strange Seas of Thought: Studies in William Wordsworth's Philosophy of Man and Nature (Bloomington: Indiana University Press, 1958.)

[9]For the Atlantic Seaboard and the Middle West, see the writings of Ralph H. Brown, C. O. Sauer, Leslie Hewes, and Hildegard Johnson. The Great Plains have been curiously ignored by geographers--perhaps because of the attention given to this region by historians like R. C. Morris, Walter Prescott Webb, and the historian of literature, Henry Nash Smith. See, however, G. M. Lewis, "Changing Emphasis in the Transactions of the Institute of British Geographers, No. 30 (1962), pp. 75-90.

subtle hints provided by landscape painting, to the less subtle hints provided by property values. The former type of evidence was used with consummate skill by Bernard Smith in his study of the European vision of the South Pacific.[10] R. L. Heathcote, on the other hand, used rent assessments as evidence of changing appraisals of the semi-arid plains of eastern Australia.[11]

Past attitudes toward nature thus reveal themselves indirectly through scattered literary sources, through the evidence perhaps of a few landscape paintings, and indirectly, through the testimony of artifacts that may have survived. There must remain a large degree of uncertainty as to the "representativeness" of the views of the few people who have left written records. In contrast, contemporary evaluations of environment can be studied not only in the deeds and writings of the active and articulate minority, but also by questioning samples of the population concerned, and by the use of psychological tests.

(5) Native cosmographies. Though curious as to frontier attitudes, geographers have, on the whole, neglected indigenous cosmographies. The views of non-literate peoples remain the concern of anthropologists, those of literate societies the concern of cultural historians. Geographers are more at home in the economics of livelihood than in the theology of belief. They are interested in evaluations of nature at the frontier, for these must be material and pragmatic if the immigrants are to survive. In long-settled areas, on the other hand, material needs grow less urgent. Nature is no longer consciously appraised for its practical uses. Cosmographic notions reveal their structures less clearly in crop and field patterns than in myths and taboos, in architectural design, and in the layout of gardens and other non-utilitarian spaces.

II

Beyond these approaches, there is another that has not yet been systematically explored. It is to delineate attitudes toward nature by focusing attention on landscapes that have acquired special symbolic significance.

The recognition and differentiation of landscapes does not seem to be an old or common human trait. Among pre- and non-literate peoples, awareness of nature gen-

---

[10] Bernard Smith, European Vision and the South Pacific, 1768-1850 (New York and London: Oxford University Press, 1960).

[11] R.L. Heathcote, "Historical Changes in the Appraisal of Pastoral Land and Resources, With Special Reference to the Semi-arid Plains of Eastern Australia," Review of Marketing and Agricultural Economics XXXI, (1963), pp. 3-23.

8

erally takes other forms. Nature is recognized, on the one hand, in local objects--individual animals, plants, and rocky prominences. On the other hand, it is perceived as generalized phenomena, as sky, moon, earth, water, light and darkness. Exceptions occur in environments of striking contrasts. Thus the Lele of Kasai are keenly aware of the differences between the forest and the grassland, which have for them more than economic significance.[12] And in the dualistic scheme of the Balinese, mountains and sea symbolize two worlds--the one upward in the direction of life, the other downward in the direction of calamity, sickness, and death.[13]

Among literate peoples, the reading of significance into arbitrarily selected spatial units of nature is also remarkably rare. The East Indians, for example, have shown little interest in landscapes--at least as far as can be judged from their visual arts.[14] The Chinese, by contrast, endow mountains and streams with distinctive meaning. In the Western tradition, although a great variety of landscapes are recognized and depicted in art, two antithetical scenes--the desert and the tropical island--have acquired special richness of meaning and emotional force. "Desert" and "tropical island" mean relatively little to the South or East Asian; they are not part of his dream world nor of his paysage moralisé.[15] But to Western man, these words evoke more than a pair of climates or vegetation types. Responses to them are likely to be varied, often contradictory. Let me sketch some of the historical roots of this diverse and intense response.

Consider first the deserts. It has often been pointed out that the Graeco-Hebraic roots of the Western tradition were established on the fringe of the greatest desert in the world. And Hebrew literature evinces keen awareness of that desolate landscape. But Greek and Roman writers, despite the perspicacity of their geographical insights in other areas, showed a remarkable capacity to overlook the deserts or, when

8

---

[12] Mary Douglas, "The Lele of Kasai," in African Worlds: Studies in the Cosmological Ideas and Social Values of African Peoples, ed. Daryll Forde (New York and London: Oxford University Press, 1954), pp. 4-7.

[13] Justus M. van der Kroef, "Dualism and Symbolic Antithesis in Indonesian Society," American Antiquity LVI (1954), p. 855.

[14] Giuseppe Tucci, "Earth in India and Tibet," Eranos-Jahrbuch 1953 (Rhein-Verlag Zürich: 1954), pp. 324-25.

[15] The desert waste does have significance for the Chinese as the scene of border wars with the Central Asiatic tribes. The border, the fortress, grass plains, and sandy wastes denote war, death, separation and loneliness. In the popular anthology, Three Hundred Poems of T'ang Dynasty, (618-906 A.D.)

they were aware of them, to minimize their extent. Neglect of the dry world in the Homeric epics is to be expected. Homer's known world was centered on the Mediterranean basin. The landscapes admired in his time were those that produced food. Libya is mentioned in the Odyssey only as a region of great fertility.[16] Later Greek writers also neglected the dry lands.

Greek neglect of the deserts can best be understood in the context of two beliefs. One was the strongly-held notion of temperature zones, interpreted on astronomical principles. Precipitation, which did not lend itself to such an interpretation, was ignored.[17] The supposed modest size of Africa was another common belief. Herodotus imagined the combined size of Africa and Asia to be far less than that of Europe.[18] The tendency to exaggerate Europe's latitudinal extent may have been encouraged by the reputation for great cold in long-colonized lands north of the Black Sea. On the other hand, Africa was assumed to terminate not far beyond the southern limit of the known regions--Ethiopia and the Land of Cinnamon. This belief appears to have endured from the time of Herodotus to that of Strabo, whose truncated Africa was about one-third of its actual size. One effect of the diminution of Africa was to diminish also its greatest desert, the Sahara, to a feature of no great prominence.

Even more curious than the neglect of the Sahara was the neglect of the smaller, more accessible Arabian desert. Bunbury saw little evidence of new knowledge of that peninsula between the time of Eratosthenes and that of Strabo, a lapse of about three centuries. The elder Pliny "in common with most other ancient writers applied the name of Arabia Felix...in a sense that would seem to comprehend almost the whole peninsula."[19] Arabia Deserta, on the other hand, was limited to the desert strip between the Gulf of Suez and the head of the Persian Gulf. The Romans, who appear to have been wholly unacquainted with the interior deserts, had highly exaggerated notions

---

(618-906 A.D.), about a dozen poems touch on the "border" theme. But there is no special emphasis on the desert as symbol of separation, isolation, and death. "Cold wind" and "snow over green grave" seem to serve that function more frequently.

[16] Odyssey IV.

[17] John Leighly, "Dry Climates: Their Nature and Distribution," Desert Research, Proceedings International Symposium, Research Council of Israel, Special Publication No. 2 (Jerusalem: 1963).

[18] Herodotus, History iv, 42.

[19] E. H. Bunbury, A History of Ancient Geography among the Greeks and Romans, (2nd ed.; New York: Dover, 1959) II, p. 426.

of the richness and fertility of Arabia.[20]

Ancient writers tended to neglect the dry lands for reasons of theology as well as cosmogony. How could these great expanses of near sterility be made to fit the view of nature inspired by the Hebraic-Christian notion of a provident and omnipotent God? This kind of question must have been raised, for answers were given. Augustine's answer was to avoid too narrow--too anthropocentric--a notion of God's providence. In the City of God he wrote: ". . .that heat which is disagreeable to them (human beings) some animals find the most suitable conditions of a healthy life."[21] On the whole, natural theology in Western Christendom developed along the lines of a liberal interpretation of Providence. The famous apologist, Paley, viewed the camel's adjustment to desert life as one of the marvels of God's providence.[22] And to the third Earl of Shaftesbury, the vast deserts themselves "want not their peculiar beautys."[23]

During the 18th century, however, another, narrower view began to predominate.[24] "Geology," wrote Murchison, "convinces us that every variation of the earth's surface has been but a step toward the accomplishment of one great end," which was to fashion the earth "into a fit abode for Man by the ordinances of Infinite Wisdom."[25] But

---

[20] Bunbury, op. cit., p. 427.

[21] Augustine City of God XII,4 (trans. Marcus Dods Edinburgh: T&T Clark, 1871).

[22] W. Paley, Natural Theology: or Evidences of the Existence and Attributes of the Deity, Collected from the Appearances of Nature (Albany: Daniel and Samuel Whiting, 1803), pp. 173-74.

[23] Third Earl of Shaftesbury, Characteristics of men, manners, opinions, times, Vol. II: An Inquiry Concerning Virtue and Merit (2nd ed.; London: 1714), p. 388.

[24] For example, Stephen Hales, Statistical Essays (London: 1731), II, vii, quoted by C. C. Gillispie, Genesis and Geology (New York: Harper, 1959), p. 12. James Hutton wrote: "The globe of this earth is evidently made for man," but only because man alone, of all creatures, is capable of enjoying intellectually, "the whole and every part." Theory of the Earth, with Proofs and Illustrations (Edinburgh: W. Creech, 1795), I, pp. 17-18.

[25] Roderick Murchison, The Silurian System (London: J. Murray, 1839), p. 575. This is the peroration at the end of Part I. The Silurian System is otherwise a straightforward work in descriptive geology. See also William Buckland, Vindiciae Geologicae (Oxford: 1820), p. 12; William Prout, Chemistry, Meteorology, and the Function of Digestion, considered with reference to Natural Religion (London: Pickering, 1834), p. 180.

if the earth was designed as the abode of man (rather than for the whole of animate creation), the inordinate size of surfaces of little use to humans had to be accounted for. The problem was answered in an indirect way. Paley[26] and Buckland[27]--like John Keill and John Ray more than a century before--considered the disproportionate size of the oceans as, in fact, necessary; smaller oceans (in their view) would not have supplied sufficient moisture to fertilize the land. That much land remained inadequately supplied with moisture was conveniently ignored. The divine and the natural philosopher were able to forget the deserts, and to be in tacit agreement with the poet Thomson, who rather imprecisely described the color green as "Nature's universal robe."[28]

The prophetic religions that originated in the dry world frequently resorted to nature for their images. Those aspects of the landscape that received persistent attention, and the symbolic uses to which they were put, reflect the attitudes of desert peoples toward their environment. The Bible abounds in references to the desert and the wilderness. Encounters with God, both directly and through prophetic voices, took place in scenes of desolation. God spoke on an empty stage, knowing how easily the sound of rivers diverted human attention. Yet when the Lord pleaded with backsliding Israel He recalled how He had led them out of a land of deserts into a plentiful country "to eat the fruit thereof." "I will even make a way in the wilderness and rivers in the desert," says the Lord (Isaiah 43:19). The deserts as such were not appreciated by the Children of Israel. They were abodes of bleak despair. The desired landscape was the garden, a land of milk and honey.

In distinction to the Bible, the Qur'an barely mentions wildernesses and deserts. The prophet preferred to emphasize the providence of God, who not only created the heavens and the earth, but also sent rain on a dead land so that it could bring forth fruit. The theme of "rain on a dead land" is repeated many times in the Qur'an. Also prominent is the theme of rewarding the faithful with Paradise, the geography of which includes many elements that desert people might desire: palm trees, shade from the sun, protection from piercing cold, fountains, running rivers. "Verily, the pious are

---

[26] Paley, op. cit., pp. 255-256.

[27] Buckland, Vindiciae Geologicae, pp. 12-13.

[28] James Thomson, The Seasons (London: 1728), I, 83. Another Scot and contemporary, James Hutton, exhibited a similar disregard for the real extent of dry lands. His Theory of Rain (1784) required very few dry spots. In fact, he acknowledged only two: Lower Egypt and the coast of Peru.

amid shades and springs and fruits such as they love" (Surah 77).

An appreciation for the desert scene in itself was perhaps first voiced by desert hermits in the 4th century A.D. The hermits went to live in the desert not, of course, for its beauty. On the contrary, it was barrenness that attracted them. The desert provided the bare surface on which one could give one's undivided attention to God. Anthony, the Egyptian hermit, even declaimed against the rising of the sun for disturbing him in his prayer.[29] And Abba Abraham commended lands that lacked fruitfulness for not distracting men with thoughts of cultivation.[30] But there is evidence that despite these biases, the hermits learned to appreciate the austere beauty of the desert as such.[31] When Jerome wrote, "to me a town is a prison, and the desert loneliness a paradise," he expressed an attitude which might well have been that of certain other hermits of his time.[32] It was, however, a point of view incongruent with Biblical sentiment, and could hardly differ more from the esthetic geography of the Qur'an.

The mood that discerned spiritual purity in a sterile landscape appears to have been but a brief epoch in the growth of Christian monasticism. Monastic life continued and reached its peak of influence in later centuries, but the deserts themselves had before then become inaccessible to Christian endeavor. For Christianized Europe, the association of dry lands with mystic beauty lacked the sustenance of actual experience. The word "desert" itself had come to mean any uninhabited area--even a forest--rather than a barren landscape.

By the 18th century, the Levant lay open once more to infidel travelers from the West; in the 19th century the desert regained, chiefly through the works of English travelers, a touch of its former transcendental significance.[33] Unlike the desert fathers, however, modern hermits sought solitude and desolation without a compensating thirst for God; in persons less vital than a Burton or a Doughty, their search

---

[29]Cassian Conferences ix. 31, trans. C.S. Gibson in Nicene and Post-Nicene Fathers (2nd. Ser.; New York: 1894), XI.

[30]Cassian Conferences xxiv, 3, 4, 12.

[31]W.H. Mackean, Christian Monasticism in Egypt (London: Society for Promoting Christian Knowledge, 1920), pp. 135-137.

[32]Jerome Letters xiv. 10, trans. W.H. Freemantle in Nicene and Post-Nicene Fathers (2nd Ser.; New York: 1893), VI.

[33]Robin Fedden, English Travellers in the Near East (Writers and Their Work No. 97), (New York: Longmans, Green and Co., 1958), p. 44.

carried misanthropic overtones. Norman Douglas, for instance, felt relief as he
looked into the salt depression of Chott in Tunisia; it pleased him that at least this
little speck of the globe was irreclaimable by potato-planters for all time.[34] For
Douglas, a "poignant little epigram. . .shall justify the existence of a myriad leagues
of useless sand, and the non-existence of several myriad useful cultivators."[35] How
superficial this mood seems beside that of Abba Abraham, who commended sandy
wastes not because of the bon mots they provoked, but because the modesty of the
deserts permitted the undivided worship of God.

Mystic and misanthropic responses to the desert are undoubtedly exceptional,
unduly prominent perhaps because so well expressed. Much more common is the
attitude that the desert is a blot to be reclaimed, made fertile and habitable. The
Biblical attitude remains the dominant one, although it is now man rather than the Lord
who says: "I will even make a way in the wilderness, and rivers in the desert."

The expression "tropical island"--to turn to the other aspect of this antithetical pair--evokes a more homogeneous emotional response than the word "desert."
The word "island" alone may call forth the image of a Garden of Eden, paradise, utopia,
or holiday camp--places that differ from each other but are alike in their remoteness
from the realities of the continent.

The message was not always so clear. In Homeric Greece, the islands of
Odysseus rose rock-like from the sea, but none of them was rich in grass. And where
an island yielded fruit, there lurked the threat of the Cyclopes. On the other hand,
archaic Greece also nurtured the legend of the Island of the Blessed, which provided
heroes with unearned harvests thrice a year.[36]

The Greek legend appears to have had Celtic parallels. Plutarch relates the
story of a Celtic island on which no one toiled; its climate was exquisite, its air
steeped in fragrance.[37] The Celtic Elysium for gods and heroes was pre-Christian in

[34] Norman Douglas, "Arabia Deserta" (an appreciation of Doughty's Arabia
Deserta), in Experiments (New York: R.M. McBride & Company, 1925). Douglas
rejoices in the news that South Africa is "sinking into unproductive desert, even as
Australia has already sunk. . . Let it sink! May it be utterly unexploitable and
uninhabitable to the crack of doom!"

[35] Douglas, op. cit., p. 21.

[36] Hesiod, Works and Days, 168; Pindar; Olympia, 2.

[37] Plutarch, Obsolescence of Oracles (De defectu oraculorum), trans. F.C.
Babbitt, 18; The faces of the Moon (De facie lunae), trans. H. Cherness, 26. Plutarch's

inspiration. In Christian Ireland, certain pagan romances were converted into edifying tales of saintly endeavor. Especially popular throughout medieval Europe was the legend of St. Brendan, in which the Abbot of Clonfort (d. 576) became a sea-faring hero who discovered insular paradises of blissful ease and abundance. In a 12th century Anglo-Norman version of the tale, Brendan was made to search for an island described idyllically as a home for the pious that lay beyond the sea, "U malls orrez nuls ne cisle, U fud pouz de cel odur que en parais gettent li flur . . ."[38] Succeeding centuries down to the 15th added to the fame of Brendan's island-Eden.[39]

During the 16th and early 17th centuries, under the stimulus of Renaissance humanism, such utopian schemes as those of Thomas More, Johann Valentin Andreae,[40] and Francis Bacon enriched island imagery. A life of ease was not a condition of these utopias, nor did they demand a tropical setting. But the view of the island as Eden, evoking nostalgia for lost innocence, has an enduring place in the Western mind. In Shakespeare's The Tempest, Gonzalo would banish all commerce, indeed all work from the island. "All things in common nature should produce without sweat or endeavor. Treason, felony, sword, pike, knife, gun, or need of any engine, would I not have; but nature should bring forth, of its own kind, all foison, all abundance, to feed my innocent people."[41] In our time, the latest Huxleyan utopia was set not only on an island, but one

---

"authority" was a Demetrius of Tarsus who may have been a Roman functionary in Britain, and who may have told Plutarch some Celtic legend which the latter hellenized and wove into the fabric of his myth. See John R. Macculoch, Celtic Mythology Vol. III of The Mythology of All Races, ed. Louis H. Gray (Boston: Marshall Jones Company, 1918), pp. 14-15, 123.

[38] "Where no tempest revels, where for nourishment one inhales the perfume of flowers from paradise." The Anglo-Norman Voyage of St. Brendan by Benedit, ed. E.G.R. Walters (New York: Oxford University Press, 1928), p. 7.

[39] W.H. Babcock, "St. Brendan's Explorations and Islands," Geographical Review, VIII (1919), pp. 39-40. The most elaborate characterization of Brendan's insular paradise occurs in the 15th century Lives of the Saints, from the Book of Lismore, edited, with a translation by Whitley Stokes (Oxford: Clarendon Press, 1890), pp. 259-60. The contrast in response between St. Anthony and St. Brendan is of interest. Anthony heard by chance the Gospel message, "If thou wishest to be perfect . . . take up thy cross, and come after Me, and there shall be unto thee treasure in heaven." He responded by retreating into the desert. Brendan heard the Gospel message, "Every one that hath forsaken father or mother or sister or lands (for my name's sake) . . . shall possess everlasting life." Unlike Anthony, Brendan responded by beseeching the Lord to give him a land that is separated from men, but "secure" and "delightful"-- in other words, a "beautiful noble island with trains of angels rising from it."

[40] Johann Valentin Andreae (1586-1654), Christianopolis: an Ideal State of the Seventeenth Century, tr. Felix Emil Held (New York: Oxford University Press, 1916).

[41] Tempest, Act II, Scene 1.

located in the permissive climate of south Asia.[42] It represents a modern withdrawal from the harshness of the Brave New World, and from the strenuous optimism of its Renaissance precursors.

Utopias are conceptually different from Edens. They depict societies which could be made ideal, thanks, in part, to limited size imposed by a narrow but diversified geographical base on an island or in a valley. Gardens of Eden, on the other hand, convey more a sense of natural abundance in which one can live in tropical ease and blissful isolation[43] beyond the reach of possible social conflict. Eden may have only two inhabitants (Robinson Crusoe and Friday), sometimes only one. Defoe's fantasy (presented, however, in naturalistic prose) was immensely popular, and inspired many imitations. One such, The Hermit (1727), claimed to give the facts concerning the life of an Englishman stranded on an uninhabited South Sea island. The almost total lack of human society over a period of fifty years did not prevent him from leading a cultivated life in Edenesque surroundings. Visitors, including the author of the book, were given a four-course dinner: thick soup, boiled meat with oyster sauce, a roast with mushrooms, and antelope cheese.[44]

This kind of island-paradise fantasy received later encouragement from scientific expeditions to the South Seas. Louis de Bougainville's Tahiti was an indubitable Eden. The voyages of Captain Cook largely confirmed the desirability of the South Sea islands. According to the naturalist George Forster, the islands' appeal to visitors may also have been greatly enhanced by what preceded the encounter, which was usually a long dreary voyage over cold and empty seas.[45]

In the 19th century, under the assaults of missionaries, tropical islands barely managed to maintain their symbolic role as gardens of Eden. Their reputation was upheld, however, by visitors like Herman Melville, Mark Twain, Robert Louis

---

[42] Aldous Huxley, Island (New York: Harper and Row, 1962).

[43] Latin insula (island)--"isolation."

[44] Walter de la Mare, Desert Islands and Robinson Crusoe (New York: Farrar and Rinehart, 1930), pp. 225-26. The Hermit: or the unparalleled (sic) Sufferings and Surprising Adventures of Mr. Philip Quarll, an Englishman; who was lately discovered by Mr. Dorrington (Peter Longueville?) a British Merchant, upon an uninhabited Island in the South Sea; where he has lived about fifty years without any human assistance, still continues to reside, and will not come away (Westminster: 1727).

[45] George Forster, A Voyage from Bengal to England. . . (London: 1777, I) pp. 124-25.

Stevenson, and Henry Adams.[46] The enjoyment of islands by visitors suggests another island connotation--that of temporary escapism. Gardens of Eden and utopias are not always taken very seriously, least of all in the 20th century. But they may be needed as make-believe. For a short period of time, the American or European on vacation allows himself to be enchanted by coconut palms and bonhomie. But like Prospero in the Tempest, he must sooner or later put away the magic and return to the stolid mainland realities of Naples, or Omaha, Nebraska.

How stands the desert against the tropical island in the Western imagination? The awesome sterility of the desert seems to negate human dreams. We ask for bread and it gives us stone. Three common attitudes toward the desert have been: to deny its existence or real extent; to transform it for human use; to seek God or transcendence in a totally exposed landscape. Of these three attitudes, 20th-century man finds the last unimportant, and has combined the first two; together with the desire to transform the desert run the beliefs that it is of no great extent and is readily transformable. The desert (excepting perhaps a pretty sand dune here and there) has never aroused protective feelings. It is subject to abuses from miner's pick to nuclear explosions without appearing much the worse for wear. The conquest of the desert, in the form of expanding cotton fields, highways, and billboards, generates only a sense of triumph. In contrast is the tropical island. It represents innocence, fertility, and ease. But it is a vulnerable paradise, one to which we introduce modern conveniences with a note of apology and with trepidation.

The patience of a geographer may be strained by the study of attitudes that appear at times only distantly related to direct terrestrial expressions. But the humanistic study of attitudes demands and repays the same attention we give to the scientific analysis of physical processes. Both approaches lie at the fringe of geography; yet neither can be ignored if we aspire to a catholic appreciation of the earth and its tenancy by man.

The study of attitudes tends to emphasize the role of fantasy in transforming nature--or in leaving nature severely alone as, in some sense, sacred. To borrow a distinction adumbrated by theologians, it depicts man's world rather than man's

---

[46]Among writers, Mark Twain was undoubtedly one of the most enthusiastic. He unblushingly called the Hawaiian islands "paradise," "blessed retreat," and "heaven." By way of contrast, he had very harsh things to say of the desert. The alkali flats west of Salt Lake City, he characterized as possessing a "concentrated hideousness that shames the diffused and diluted horrors of Sahara." Roughing It (New York: Harper, 1913), I, p. 149.

environment. Man's world is a fabric of ideas and dreams, some of which he manages to give visible form. For the privilege of having fantasies, of possessing a world rather than simply an environment, man pays with the risk of disaster and the certainty of ultimate impermanence in all his efforts. Montgomery's Azilia has substance only on paper. The faith of New Mexico's pinto-bean farmers leaves visible but precarious traces on a dry land. The Mormons, in comparison, have imposed a firmer imprint on Utah. These and other works of man may be seen as reified fantasies; fantasies that have acquired varying degrees of transient substance through the ingenuity and stubbornness of our more practical dreamers.

CHAPTER II

SPATIAL MEANING, AND THE PROPERTIES OF THE ENVIRONMENT

Robert Beck

Perception of the environment requires man to interpret the physical and social components of his stimulus field. Such an area of inquiry falls congruently into the disciplines of geography and psychology, which are concerned, respectively, with the physical properties of the stimulus field and with personal attributes arising out of functional and symbolic transactions between men and that field. These transactions further lead to the establishment of group attitudes, beliefs, and values associated with various domains of the environmental field. The physical and interpersonal properties of the environment are distributed in space, and personal environmental space is shaped by the configuration of these properties. Personal systems of spatial meaning may yield important insights into individual perceptions of the environment.

The theory of spatial meaning includes insights from many disciplines. It requires some consideration of the philosophy and logic of space. The question, "Is space inherently or experientially derived?" must be answered before questions concerning developmental spatial articulation can even be formulated. That space is personal and has unique meaning for the individual is clear from the existential-psychiatric literature on the psychopathology of experienced space, and from the brilliant spatial-phenomenological speculations of such men as Binswanger,[1] Straus,[2] and Minkowski.[3] The work of artists, art critics, and anthropologists likewise yield categories important for an interpretation of space in psychological terms. The painter,

---

[1] Ludwig Binswanger, "Traum und Existenze," in his Ausgewahlte Vorhage uns Aufsatze, Bern, A. Flancke, 1947.

[2] Erwin Straus, The Primary World of Senses, tr. Jacob Needleman (Glencoe, Illinois: Free Press, 1963).

[3] Eugene Minkowski, Le Temps vécu (Paris, 1939).

18

the sculptor, the architect, the city planner, are all professional manipulators of the spatial field, translators of spatial meaning into tangible structures, their systems of spatial terminologies are invaluable in the study of spatial meaning. The linguistic spatial expressions and notation systems of other cultures may also be tapped as sources of a spatial grammar.

In the developmental articulation of the self with environment, and the subsequent differentiation of the environment itself into increasingly discrete and heterogeneous parts, percept and concept are conjoined. Each of the sensory modalities breaks down phenomena into sets of components. The progressive delineation of forms in space is a basic part of this process. Spatial reference and orientation systems--for example, up-down, left-right, horizontal-vertical, dense-diffuse, open-delineated, forward-backward, near-far, symmetrical-asymmetrical--are not mere geometrical abstractions, but meaningful properties of individual environments. The six cardinal directions are not endowed with equivalent meaning for us; up and down, front and back, left and right, have particular values because we happen to be a special kind of bilaterally symmetrical terrestrial animal. As Lowenthal has stated, "It is one contingent fact about the world that we attach very great importance to things having their tops and bottoms in the right places; it is another contingent fact that we attach more importance to their having fronts and backs in the right places than their left and right sides."[4] In fact, people adapt more rapidly to distorting spectacles that invert up and down than to those that invert right and left.

The spatial field is differentially charged with meaning from individual to individual; and particular configurations of the spatial field may be important clues to personality. As a sacred grove has historical-religious significance for a whole people, so individuals acquire and integrate spatial axes and orientations which become personal styles. Spatial styles are analogous to characteristic conceptual, expressive, and other personal styles, which are built word upon word, action upon action. Such styles are carried as unique personality attributes. As these spatial styles become more and more a part of the personality structure of the individual, space is slowly divided into definitive zones and directions with intuitive meanings and an expressive character of their own.

Whole cultures, through the use of myth, render certain spatial configurations

---

[4] David Lowenthal, "Geography, Experience and Imagination: Towards a Geographical Epistemology," Annals of the Association of American Geographers, LI (1961) pp. 241-260.

20

distinct and important. According to Cassirer,[5] "Myth arrives at spatial determi-
nations and differentiations only by lending a peculiar mythical accent to each 'region'
in space, to the 'here' and 'there', the rising and setting of the sun, the 'above' and
'below'." In Greece, myth flooded, embraced the relation of man and land, the
meaning the land had for him. To quote Scully:

> . . . not only were certain landscapes indeed regarded by the Greeks
> as holy and expressive of certain Gods, or rather as embodiments of
> their presence, but . . . the temples and the subsidiary buildings of their
> sanctuaries were so formed in themselves, and so placed in relation to
> the landscape and to each other as to enhance, develop, and sometimes
> even contradict, the basic meaning that was felt in the land . . . There-
> fore, no study of Greek temples can be purely morphological, of form
> without theme . . . since in Greek art, the two are one. The form is
> the meaning.[6]

Let us return to the development of spatial meaning and its relation to the
geographical environment. As meaning is acquired, it clothes the perceptual world.
The infant's active exploration of his physical environment--pushing, pulling, grasping,
thrusting--endows space with a primitive concrete meaning. But the infant passes
through stages of involvement with different kinds of space. At first the baby is placed
on his stomach (facing down), then on his back (facing up).[7] In the crawling stage, the
infant lives in the horizontal plane--his line of sight and mode of exploration is highly
uniplanar, action occurs toward and away from objects at his own level of height.

Later the child raises his head, and eventually stands up; he enters the space
of the vertical plane--up and down become coordinated, right and left gain more freedom. As the child structures space and forms object relations, innumerable spatial
connotations develop. About the same time the acquisition of binocular vision expands
the two-dimensional into the three-dimensional world. The distinction of symmetrical
from non-symmetrical relations comes later still.

The concrete primitive meaning of physical exploration is supplemented and
elaborated by the use and function of objects. Meaning is derived from a satisfaction
of needs, needs which have spatial qualities. Food-objects, tool-objects, danger-
objects and pleasure or love objects acquire special significance for the child. Mother

---

[5] Ernst Cassirer, The Philosophy of Symbolic Forms, (New Haven: Yale University Press, 1953).

[6] Vincent Scully, The Earth, The Temple and the Gods (New Haven: Yale University Press, 1962), p. 22.

[7] This will vary, of course, with the child-rearing practices of a particular culture.

is too close or far away; food is consumed (put inside or spit out); tools move, are used in certain directions--they dig in, they move vertically, horizontally; one maintains distance from or is curiously attracted toward fire, punishment, danger.

Concepts of spatial meaning thus derive from individual modes and styles of perception. Indeed, meaning and perception are inseparable. Allport has summarized the Brunswik-Ames concept of perception as "the process of apprehending probable significances. . . . Basic to the process is the fact that the organism has built up certain assumptions about the world in which it lives. These assumptions which are largely unconscious lead to . . . the attaching of significances to cues."[8]

We do, in fact, build up "assumptions," expectancies of the world which lead to meaning systems; but these meaning systems are derived from a particular kind of world. "Kind" refers to the dominant geographical-spatial construction of the environment. Each people is exposed to a unique spatial environment; for example, the world of one population may be predominantly vertical, that of another horizontal, and this verticality or horizontality becomes the dominant source for spatial assumptions.

The study of spatial distributions, real and perceived, is the cornerstone of investigations of interactions between humans and their physical environments. "The perception of what has been called space is the basic problem of all perception," as Gibson remarks. "Space perception is . . . the first problem to consider, without a solution for which the other problems remain unclear."[9]

There are three basic kinds of space. Objective space is the space of physics and mathematics, measured by universal standards along dimensions of distance, size, shape, and volume. Ego space (these are the operations of the ego which make logical objective space) is the individual's adaptation of observed to objective space, to produce a coherent and logically consistent view of sizes, shapes, and distances. Immanent space is inner, subjective space, the space of the unconscious, of dreams, of fantasy; it includes the spatial styles and orientations of the individual, and the ingrained spatial notation systems of whole cultures. This is the basic space imposed upon us by the anatomy of our bodies. Consequently, it is also the space involved in the image of our body.

---

[8] Gordon W. Allport, Becoming: Basic considerations for a Psychology of Personality (New Haven, Yale University Press, 1955).

[9] James J. Gibson, Perception of the Visual World (Boston, Houghton-Mifflin, 1950).

Spatial styles, like any other attributes of personality, are the result of prolonged and complex exchanges between the individual and his environment, --and hence derive from all three kinds of space defined above. For experimental convenience, spatial typologies may be broken down into a number of simple dichotomous variables, of which five are considered below:

1. Diffuse Space vs. Dense Space. Diffuse space has a spread apart, scattered quality; dense space suggests compactness, compression, smaller distances between objects.

2. Delineated vs. Open Space. Delineated space refers to bounded, constricted, contained, contracted, or centripetal space; open space suggests inward and outward movement, spatial penetration, liberty, and freedom.

3. Verticality vs. Horizontality. These are vectors in different spatial planes.

4. Right and Left in the Horizontal Plane. These are the two vectors of the horizontal plane.

5. Up and Down in the Vertical Plane. These are the two vectors of the vertical plane.

Personal spatial systems may be observed through preferences expressed for symbols representing individual spatial parameters. A recent study[10] employs a Spatial Symbols Test, in which pairs of figures composed of simple geometrical shapes, points, and lines, represent the five dichotomous variables described above. Subjects were asked to choose the symbol figure they prefer or like better of each of 67 pairs. (Appendix: Spatial Symbols Test).

The Spatial Symbols Test was administered to 611 subjects. Table II-1 shows the distribution of responses by age and by profession. The younger subjects were drawn from suburban grammar, junior high, and high schools in the Midwest. Professional psychologists and social workers, including students, were from academic institutions throughout the United States. A factor analysis of the entire sample indicates that five principal clusters of variables accounted for 83 percent of the variance of preference response. Table II-2 shows the item makeup of each cluster and the degree of inter-item correlation within each cluster. The number of test items used is reduced from 67 to 50; that is, 17 items are not related to any of the clusters. And, each cluster is composed of items representative of a single predicted spatial parameter.

To determine if developmental processes, as hypothesized, were influential in the acquisition of spatial styles, factor analyses were performed on each age and professional group. The results are present in Table II-3. (The number of clusters which

---

[10] Robert Beck, "A Comparative Study of Spatial Meaning," (unpublished Master's thesis, University of Chicago, 1964).

TABLE II-1

DISTRIBUTION OF THE TOTAL SAMPLE

Age Group (yrs.)	N
5 – 6	66
9 – 10	66
13 – 14	57
17 – 18	58
	247

Professional Group	N
Academic Psychologists	28
Placement Psychologists	31
Student Psychologists	172
Academic Social Workers	05
Placement Social Workers	15
Student Social Workers	94
Geographers	19
	364

Total Population = 611

TABLE II-2

FACTOR ANALYSIS OF THE TOTAL POPULATION
(N = 611)

	Factor I			Factor III	
Item Number	Correlation	Scale	Item Number	Correlation	Scale
		Diffuse-			Horizontal-
03	-.60	Dense	08	-.46	Vertical
06	-.58	"	16	-.30	"
11	-.57	"	21	-.34	"
14	-.32	"	27	-.28	"
18	-.61	"	34	-.29	"
23	-.42	"	37	-.39	"
25	-.72	"	41	-.59	"
29	-.76	"	44	-.57	"
31	-.47	"	61	-.56	"
40	-.63	"	67	-.65	"
43	-.68	"			
46	-.68	"		Factor IV	
48	-.64	"			
52	-.53	"	04	-.40	Left-Right
58	-.57	"	07	-.35	"
64	-.63	"	12	-.24	"
66	-.57	"	30	-.31	"
	Factor II		36	-.40	"
		Open-	45	-.54	"
10	.45	Delineated	50	-.57	"
15	.35	"	56	-.63	"
17	.49	"	59	-.25	"
24	.37	"			
26	.41	"		Factor V	
28	.35	"			
33	.32	"	09	-.40	Up-Down
38	.32	"	13	-.29	"
47	.29	"	22	-.30	"
49	.36	"	35	-.40	"
55	.56	"	53	-.34	"
62	.75	"	63	-.33	"

TABLE II-3

FACTOR COMPOSITION IN SUB-POPULATIONS OF THE SAMPLE

Group	Number of Factors	Composition	
5-6	2	Factor I:	8 items Left-Right 5 items Open-Delineated 4 items Horizontal-Vertical 2 items Dense-Diffuse 2 items Up-Down
		Factor II:	3 items Up-Down 3 items Horizontal-Vertical 2 items Left-Right 2 items Dense-Diffuse 1 item Open-Delineated
9-10	3	Factor I:	15 items Diffuse-Dense 4 items Open-Delineated 1 item Horizontal-Vertical
		Factor II:	7 items Left-Right 3 items Up-Down 2 items Horizontal-Vertical 1 item Dense-Diffuse
		Factor III:	5 items Left-Right 4 items Up-Down
13-14	5	Factor I:	17 items Dense-Diffuse
		Factor II:	10 items Open-Delineated
		Factor III:	9 items Left-Right
		Factor IV:	7 items Up-Down
		Factor V:	9 items Horizontal-Vertical
17-18	5	Factor I:	16 items Dense-Diffuse
		Factor II:	8 items Left-Right
		Factor III:	7 items Open-Delineated
		Factor IV:	8 items Horizontal-Vertical
		Factor V:	5 items Up-Down
Social Workers	5	Conforms to scale	
Psychologists	5	Conforms to scale	
Geographers	5	Conforms to scale	

which emerge increases from 5 to 13 years.) The clusters which appear at 5-6 years are composed of items coming from all five spatial scales. It appears that spatial preferences at this age belie an undifferentiated spatial meaning. In short, our five differentiated parameters are seen by young children as fused into a single system. Of the 32 items composing the two clusters, 22 represent the spatial planes (Left-Right; Up-Down; Horizontal-Vertical). This is in line with Cassirer's[11] hypothesis that left and right and up and down represent the child's first spatial differentiation, and the Piaget and Inhelder[12] formulation that topological space precedes projective space in development.

At 9-10 years, the item clusters increase from two to three. Two clusters are now dominated by items coming from a single scale. Spatial differentiation is increasing, and this age is marked by the appearance of an essentially Diffuse-Dense cluster, perhaps a spatial signal of the development of object relations, of an increasing sense of self as distinct from other. When the 9-10 population is divided by sex, the males largely resemble the younger population, while the females, perhaps because of their earlier physical maturation, conform more to the 13-14 year old group. By the age of 13, 5 clusters appear, each composed of items from a single scale. Now space is fully differentiated, relevant and meaningful.

Spatial experience apparently leads to differentiated spatial meaning. If this is the case, a sample of geographers might be expected to display unusual ability to differentiate space. The factor analysis of geographers' responses to the Spatial Symbols test (see Table II-4), includes the only bipolar factors (4 and 5) to appear in any population tested. This indicates that in two kinds of spatial items, Left-Right and Up-Down, geographers commonly reverse reference point and variant--they are apt to see an item otherwise considered Left as constituting Right, and items generally chosen as Up as constituting Down, and vice versa. In dealing with spatial planes, geographers are either capable of differentiating space to a finer degree than any other tested group, or are unable to make any stable discriminations--a spatial-occupational hazard!

Finally, what is the meaning of spatial symbol choices, as indicated by preference for one pole or the other within each scale? Scale means and standard deviations for our three professional groups are presented in Table II-5. (Within each

---

[11] Cassirer, op. cit.

[12] Jean Piaget and Barbel Inhelder, The Child's Conception of Space, translation F.J. Langdon and J.L. Lunzer (London: Routledge and Kegan Paul, 1956).

TABLE II-4

FACTOR ANALYSIS OF THE GEOGRAPHERS

Factor I			Factor III		
Item Number	Correlation	Scale	Item Number	Correlation	Scale
03	.62	Diffuse-Dense	08	-.55	Horizontal-Vertical
06	.55	"	16	-.46	"
11	.58	"	21	-.58	"
14	.71	"	27	-.39	"
18	.43	"	34	-.63	"
23	.36	"	37	-.77	"
25	.70	"	41	-.41	"
29	.82	"	44	-.82	"
31	.85	"	61	-.66	"
40	.65	"	67	-.55	
43	.45	"	**Factor IV**		
46	.56	"			
48	.62	"	04	+.83	Left-Right
52	.67	"	07	-.35	"
64	.91	"	30	-.40	"
66	.73	"	32	+.82	"
Factor II			42	+.76	"
			45	-.63	"
10	.44	Open-Delineated	65	+.34	"
15	.35	"	**Factor V**		
17	.52	"	01	-.29	Up-Down
24	.61	"	09	-.40	"
26	.31	"	19	+.35	"
28	.54	"	35	+.38	"
33	.71	"	39	+.39	"
38	.60	"	53	-.40	"
47	.39	"	37	+.68	"
49	.47	"	60	+.35	"
55	.75	"			
62	.62	"			

TABLE II-5

SCALE MEANS AND STANDARD DEVIATIONS IN THREE PROFESSIONAL GROUPS

		Total Population	Psychologists Stud.	Psychologists Faculty	Psychologists Professionals	Social Workers Stud.	Social Workers Faculty	Social Workers Professionals	Geographers
Diffuse	Mean	10.37	9.86	12.21	10.65	11.40	10.32	10.00	12.58
	S.D.	4.38	4.12	3.54	4.10	4.60	4.15	3.00	4.30
Open	Mean	5.32	6.30	8.23	7.50	4.90	4.15	4.00	4.32
	S.D.	2.15	2.11	2.25	2.34	2.38	2.02	1.50	2.21
Horizontal	Mean	5.32	4.32	5.25	5.30	5.70	5.05	5.00	5.68
	S.D.	2.28	2.15	2.50	2.37	2.45	1.86	1.00	3.13
Down	Mean	2.57	2.51	3.15	3.04	2.60	3.18	3.00	3.00
	S.D.	1.23	1.62	2.25	1.83	.99	1.05	1.50	.94
Left	Mean	3.28	2.97	2.42	2.55	3.00	3.80	4.00	3.74
	S.D.	1.62	1.54	1.60	1.31	1.84	1.72	2.00	1.48

profession, the Spatial Symbols Test discriminates between students and the academic-professional group, and in some instances between the academics and professionals.) Geographers exhibit <u>very strong</u> preferences for Diffuse, Delineated, and Right, but are rather ambivalent with regard to Up vs. Down and Horizontal vs. Vertical. On the Diffuse-Dense and Open-Delineated scales their scores are grossly and significantly different from the rest of the population. They have the highest preference for Horizontal of any group except social worker students. Geographers' ambivalence for Up vs. Down is augmented by the low score scatter (S.D. = .94). Geographers' preference for Left is not unlike the rest of the population (psychologists excepted).

Beyond this brief summary, little can be added. The cognitive and personality correlates of the scales are still in doubt. There is, as yet, no analysis of cross-validating materials. It is abundantly clear that different professions, age groups, and sexes approach and use spatial variables in significantly varying ways, and hence have differing spatial styles as defined here. But the psychological meaning of space is yet to be determined, and spatial approaches to the perception of the environment require greater elaboration and further classification.

SPATIAL SYMBOLS TEST

Please mark your answers to the test on the special answer sheet provided.

DO NOT MARK ON THE TEST ITSELF.

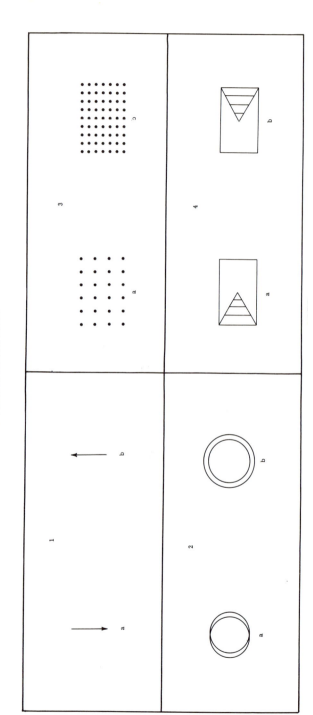

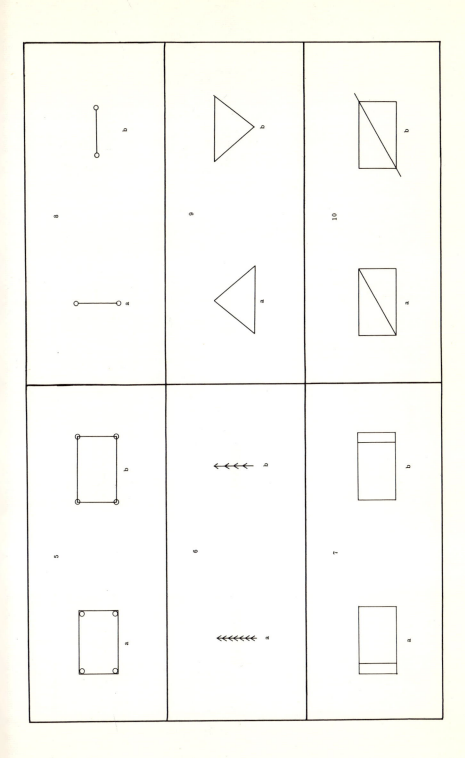

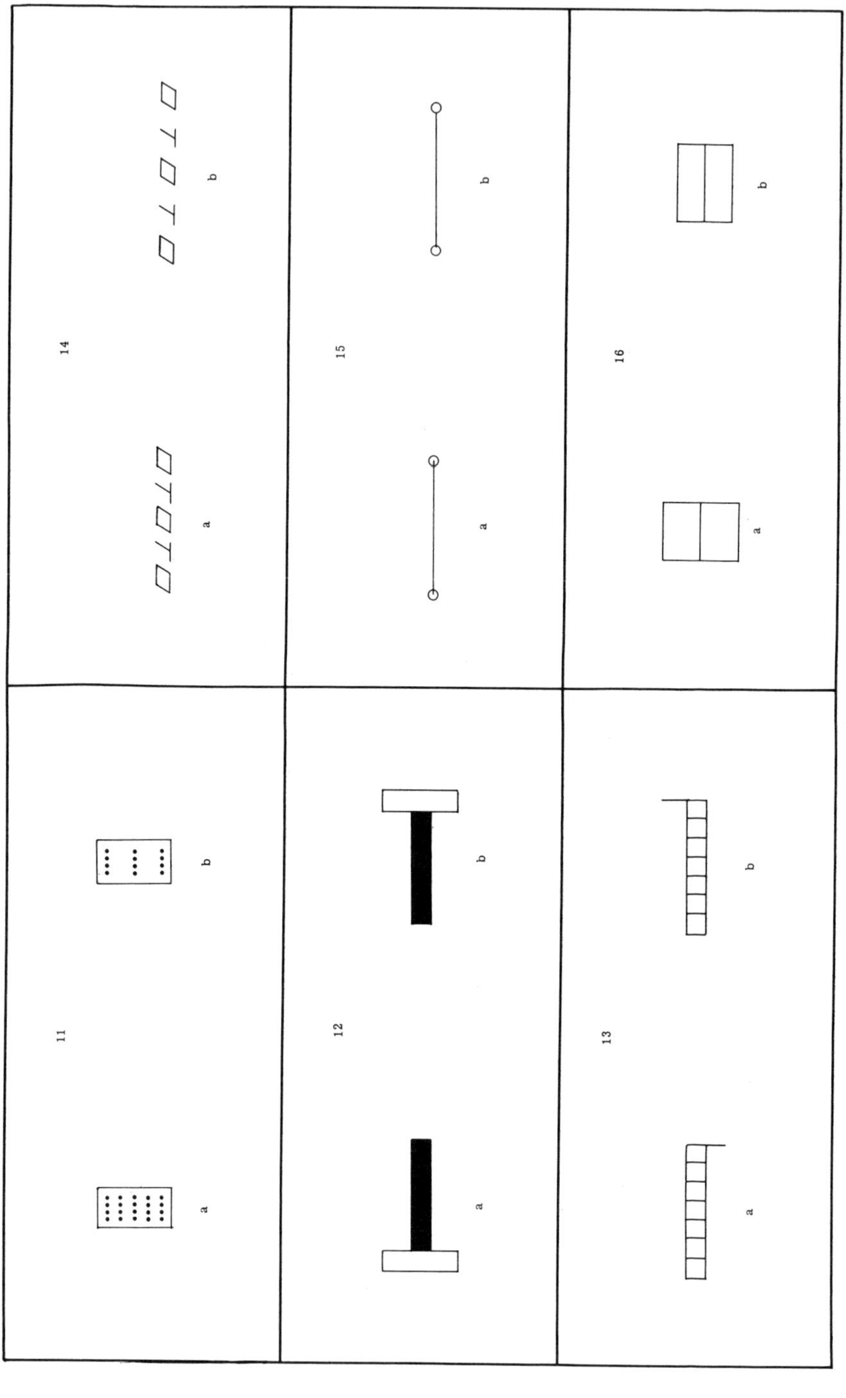
11
a
b
12
a
b
13
a
b
14
a
b
15
a
b
16
a
b

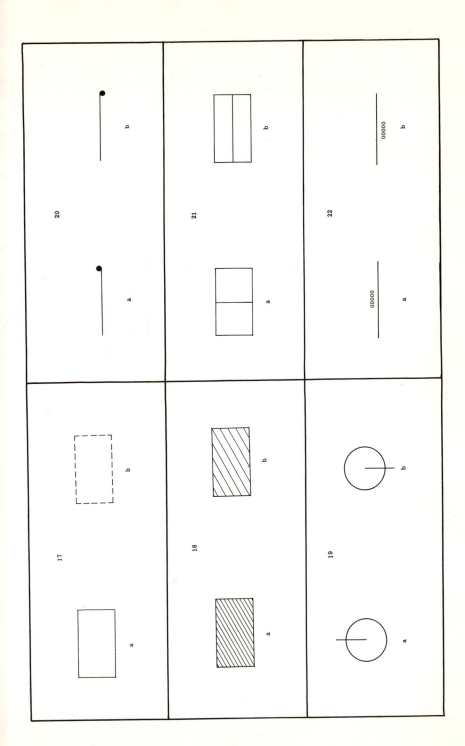

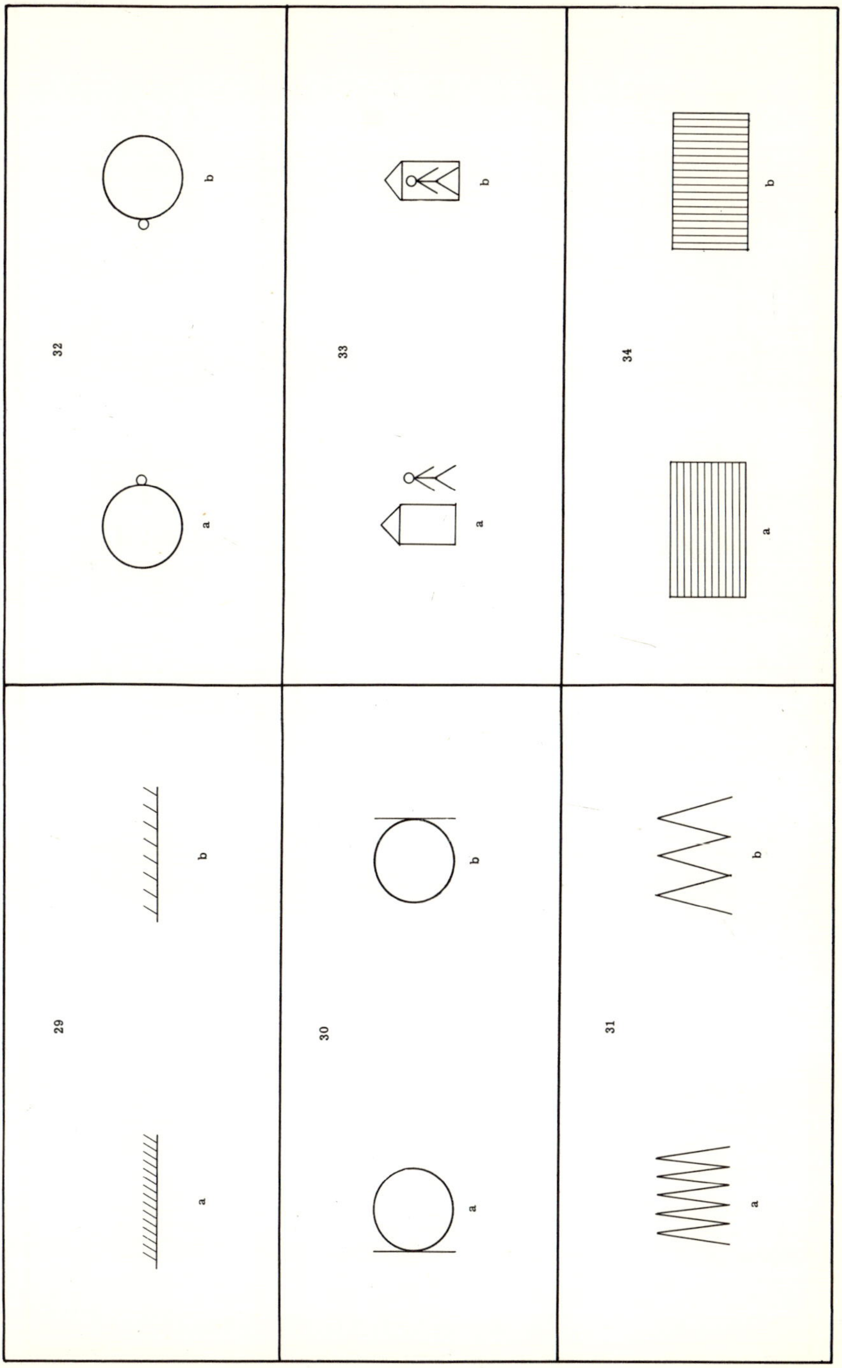
29
a
b
30
a
b
31
a
b
32
a
b
33
a
b
34
a
b

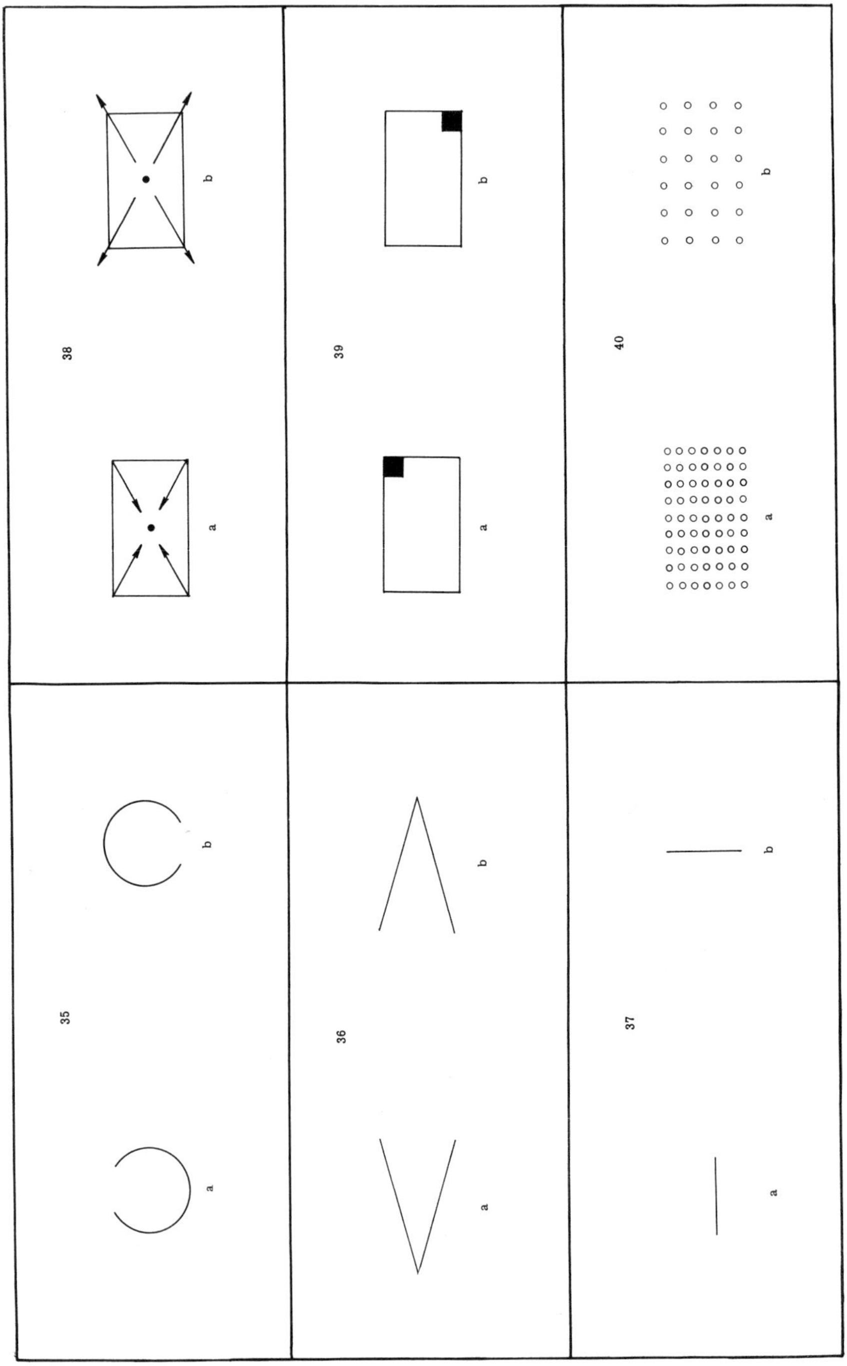
38
a
b
39
a
b
40
a
b
35
a
b
36
a
b
37
a
b

41 a b
42 a b
43 a b
44 a b
45 a b
46 a b

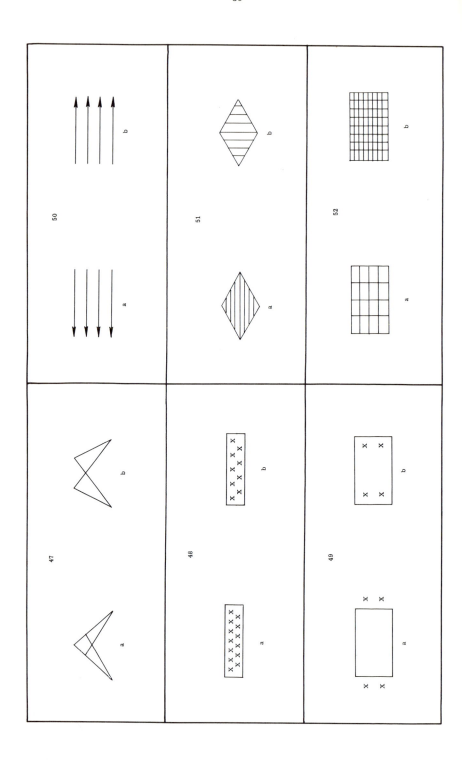

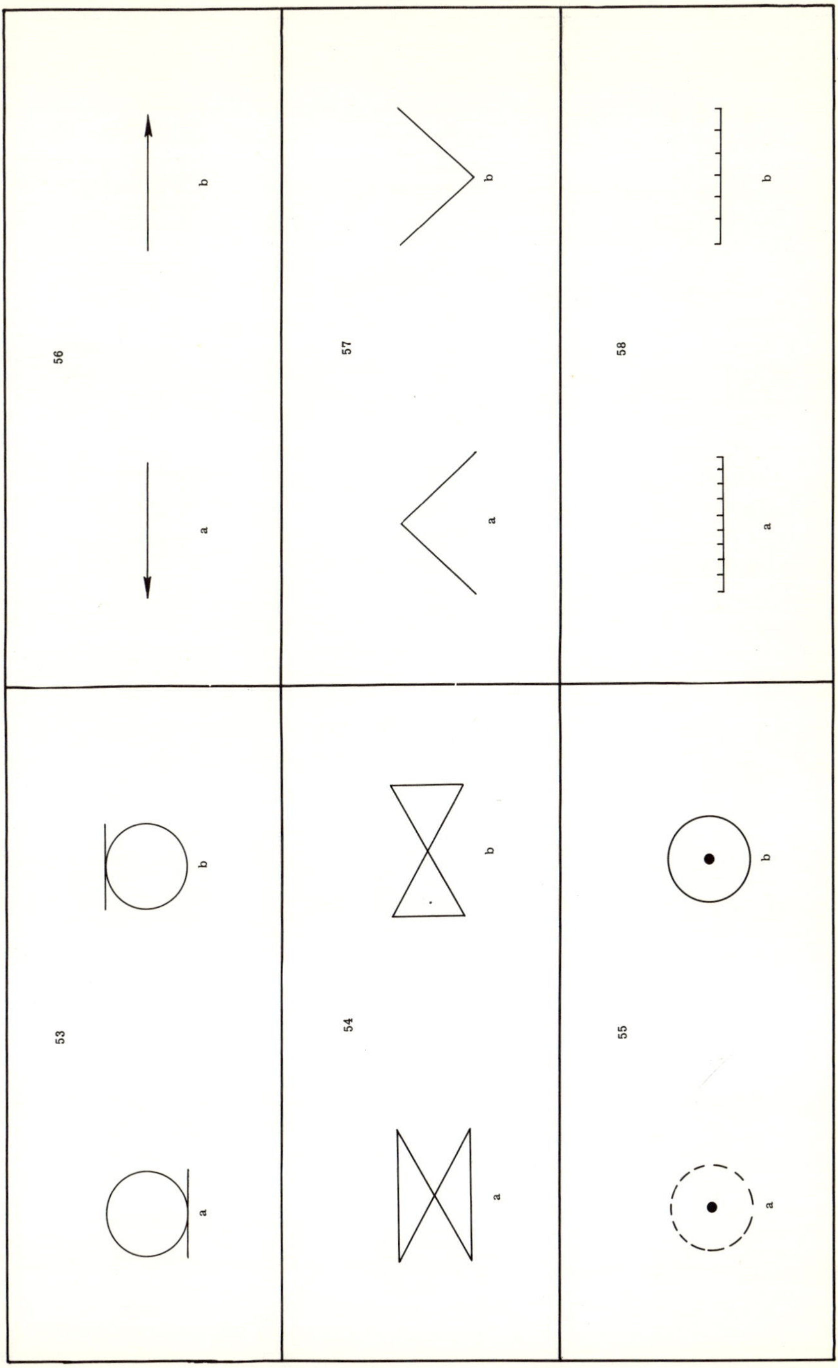
56
a
b
57
a
b
58
a
b
53
a
b
54
a
b
55
a
b

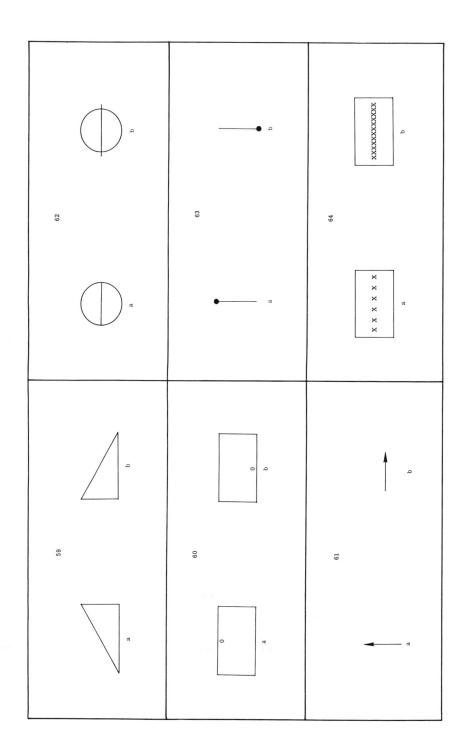

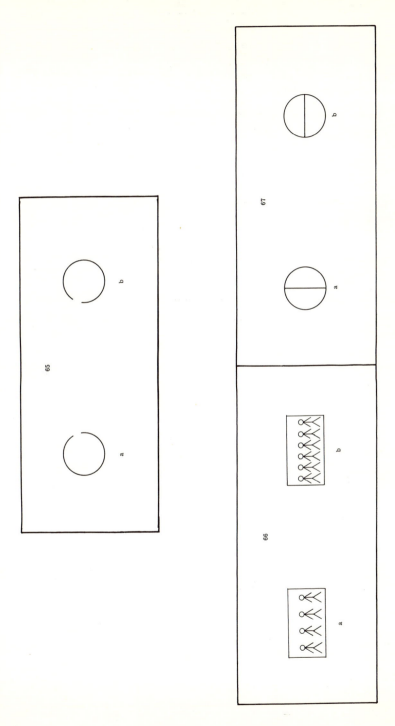

CHAPTER III

ENVIRONMENTAL PERCEPTION AND ADAPTATION
LEVEL IN THE ARCTIC[1]

Joseph Sonnenfeld

Individuals and populations tend to differ in their responses to any environment. Some achieve more in environment, some achieve less; some adjust easily to environmental extremes, others adjust only with difficulty. Different responses may be a function of different abilities to respond to environment, or of different perceptions of environment. Understanding of the sources of variance in environmental perception is essential to an understanding of variation in man's environmental behaviors.

One significant source of perceptual differences is man's variable sensitivity to environment. The concept of adaptation level here offers an invaluable tool.[2] Our bodies are capable of adjusting to environment in many ways, as physiological functioning requires. When exposed to heat or cold or high altitude, homeostatic adjustments permit the body to maintain fitness under a wide range of conditions. But the adjustment to environment is not only physiological; there is also a sensory adaptation. The individual becomes more sensitive to those new environmental conditions which require him to be sensitive, and conversely, less sensitive in circumstances where high levels of sensitivity are valueless or even disadvantageous for comfort and well-being.

While homeostatic adjustment in response to environment is a function of the interaction between a universal stimulus and the physiological organism, adaptation level involves much more. The many factors that condition the sensing and perception

[1]Data for this paper are derived from a study supported by the Arctic Institute of North America under contractual arrangements with the Office of Naval Research. Reproduction in whole or in part permitted for any purpose of the United States Government.

[2]Harry Helson, Adaptation-Level Theory (New York: Harper and Row, 1964).

of environmental stimuli also influence adaptation level, just as adaptation level subsequently influences perception. In any environment, for example, a variety of
background stimuli will condition the perception of the focal stimulus: a given relief
feature is perceived as more or less rugged according to the surrounding terrain; a
given temperature or weather condition is perceived as more or less extreme according
to the season of occurrence. Organismic variables also influence the perception of the
environmental stimulus. The perceiver's physiological and mental state varies over
both short and long time periods. Stimulus meaning and stimulus memory differ from
individual to individual. The perception of a stimulus as difficult, significant, dangerous or however else it is perceived is a function of culture, economy, personality, and
experience as well as of individual and racial physiology; all of these will condition
adaptation level, which, in turn, will determine the individual's subsequent sensitivity
to that stimulus.

Homeostatic responses, then, are universal responses to universal environmental stimuli: deficiencies of heat, oxygen, and water elicit generally universal
physiological responses, if not universally successful responses. Adaptation levels, by
contrast, are quite variable, given their basis in complex environment, experience,
culture, and personality.

The reasons for elaborating on this distinction between homeostasis and
adaptation level derive from my recent study of environmental perception among
northern Alaskan populations. When different populations appear to be differently
adapted to an extreme environment, the question of possible racial or physiological
differences is always at issue. Certain physical or physiological differences between
the races do suggest differential abilities to adjust organically to Arctic cold. But this
is only one of the many possible reasons for different population responses to the Arctic.
Technology, for one, can influence considerably the effect of Arctic stressors on the
individual and his activities; in this sense, some arctic populations have accommodated
better than others to an environment for which no human physiology is adequate. There
are, in addition, a variety of social, cultural, and psychological problems involved in
adapting to the Arctic. These appear significant not only for alien populations, but for
native populations as well. Some nonnative populations do well in the Arctic; some do
not. Similarly, the Eskimo, despite their high level of physiological and technological
adaptation, are by no means universally contented in their relationship with the Arctic
environment. What is the basis for judging success in adaptation? How does one determine the level of contentment of different populations, which is one indicator of adaptation level, and perhaps a crucial one for determining the success of both native and

nonnative populations in adapting to the Arctic.

Over the past several years, I have been trying to develop a means for studying environmental sensitivities, attitudes and preferences. The Arctic study is part of a broader cross-cultural/cross-environmental study in environmental perception that in time will be extended to other than Arctic environments and cultures. The basic tool used in this study has been the questionnaire. Those developed for studying different populations have been of varying complexity, both in the detail and diversity of environmental attitudes and sensitivities for which they probed, and in the devices used for measuring these. The data obtained from most of these questionnaires relate to personal details of age, occupation, ethnic origins, and environmental and residential experiences; to conscious physical and mental comfort and capacities or disabilities under different environmental conditions; recollections of childhood environments; current sensitivities and climatic preferences (the major portion of the questionnaire); sensitivity to climatic change; and attitudes concerning the influence of environment on man, the predictability of environment, and the desirability of changing environment. The questionnaires were designed to elicit not only the range of conscious environmental preferences and sensitivities, but also possible reasons for these in terms of distinctive physiology, experience, and personality.

In addition to the questionnaire, two other tests were developed. One utilizing semantic differentials (a technique widely used by psychologists[3]) measures the dimension of meaning of concepts representing both universal and locally experienced environmental phenomena (e.g. wind, storms, seasons, Northern Lights). In this test, each concept is rated by paired polar adjectives, such as like/dislike, common/ uncommon, hot/cold, and safe/dangerous, on a five-point scale (e.g., hot 2-1-0-1-2 cold). The test used in Alaska included fifteen concepts representing the physical environment (each rated along a set of twenty-five scales), and thirteen concepts referring to a variety of Arctic animals, meant to represent biotic environment (each rated along a different set of sixteen scales). It was administered to approximately 150 Eskimo youngsters at three villages: Barrow, which contains a group of acculturated Eskimo of coastal and inland origins, many of them recent migrants; Wainwright, which is made up of a more subsistence-oriented and homogeneous group of coastal Eskimo; and Anaktuvuk Pass, a village occupied by a unique group of inland Eskimo, for whom caribou hunting still provides an important source of subsistence. The results, it is

---

[3]See C.E. Osgood, G.J. Suci, and P.H. Tannenbaum, The Measurement of Meaning (Urbana, Illinois: University of Illinois Press, 1957).

hoped, will yield a kind of environmental profile for each of the populations, to provide a basis for comparing them not only qualitatively, but, given measurable differences,
quantitatively as well.[4]

Finally, a photo-slide test was developed, in which pictorial concepts substi-
tute for the verbal concepts of the semantic differential test; in a sense, this comes the
closest of all the tests to dealing with the problem of variability in the perception of
real world phenomena.

The remainder of this paper discusses some of the results yielded by the photo-
slide test, the first of the tests analyzed for which summary data are available for a
wide variety of Arctic and non-Arctic populations.

The photo-slide test involves pairs of slides showing, for the most part, a
variety of natural landscapes. Some fifty pairs of slides were obtained from the set of
visual aids used with the first edition of Arthur W. Strahler's Physical Geography.[5]
The landscapes depicted by the slides varied on one or more of four basic dimensions--
topography, water, vegetation, and temperature. The slides were so paired that choice
of one or the other would provide a measure of the subject's preference on one or more
of the basic dimensions. A group of three judges, myself included, established values
for the slides, based on whether the landscape depicted indicated greater or lesser
relief, richer or poorer vegetation, more or less water, or warmer or cooler temper-
atures than the slide with which each was paired. Each slide was then rated on a three-
point scale for each of the four dimensions (a "1" indicating, for a given slide, less
relief, less water, poorer vegetation, lower temperature in comparison with features
depicted by the slide with which it was paired; a "2" indicating no significant difference
between the slides paired on a given dimension; and a "3" indicating greater relief,
more water, richer vegetation, higher temperature).

This slide test was given to Eskimo adults at Barrow, Wainwright, and
Anaktuvuk Pass; to Eskimo youngsters and their teachers in elementary and junior high
schools in those villages; to scientists, technicians, and other staff of the Arctic
Research Laboratory at Barrow; to an Army Special Forces group on a short training
mission in the Arctic; to employees of one of the DEW-line stations near Barrow; and to

---

[4]Some ninety junior high school students at Newark, Delaware, were given
essentially this same test, so that the Eskimo responses could be compared with those
of a technologically developed non-Arctic population for whom environment has little
meaning in terms of subsistence.

[5]Arthur W. Strahler, Physical Geography (New York: Wiley and Co., 1951).

college and junior high school students in Delaware.[6] The photo-slide test proved
especially useful as a cross-cultural tool since it could be used among respondents
unfamiliar with the English language; many of the Eskimo adults, even those at so
acculturated a place as Barrow, use English awkwardly, if at all. The instructions to
all groups were essentially the same: if the respondent had to live for a year or two at
one of the places depicted by the pair of slides projected, which one of the two would he
prefer.

Indices were computed for each individual on thirteen dimensions, based on the
sum of the values of those slides chosen.[7] Population summaries were obtained for
some 200 sub-groups distinguished for the most part by age, sex, village, environmental experience, marital status, and occupation. "T-tests" were carried out to
determine significance of the difference between population means on the various dimensions. In addition, contingency tables were derived and Chi-squares calculated to help
determine the significance of specific slide choices. An IBM 1620 computer was used
for obtaining individual indices on the thirteen dimensions, population summaries and
Chi-squares.

Feedback from respondents suggested certain differences that were likely to
emerge. Eskimo sought indications of game or good hunting; women looked for fuel
materials; a soil scientist looked for places he hadn't yet been that might contain soils
he hadn't yet sampled; investigators on extended tours at Barrow looked for trees or
indications of warmer climes; members of the Army Special Forces group looked for
terrain containing protective cover. Working hypotheses were based in part on test
feedback and in part on previous responses to climatic attitude questionnaires. It
seemed reasonable to expect, first, that Eskimo from the different villages would
prefer different kinds of topography: those from Anaktuvuk Pass, the more rugged
landscapes, those from Barrow, the more level. The group from Wainwright, coast-
ally oriented but familiar with inland activities and environments, was expected to be
intermediate between the other two.

Secondly, I expected male-female differences, based on differences in subsistence concern--male the hunter, female the homemaker and fuel-gatherer, but with

---

[6]Junior high school students were tested because Eskimo schools in the
Alaskan villages generally do not extend beyond the 8th grade.

[7]The thirteen scores obtained represented primary scores for (1) topography,
(2) water, (3) vegetation, and (4) temperature, in addition to secondary scores for
each of these on slide pairs with some other primary dimension.

a greater discrepancy between male and female among the more acculturated, wage-oriented Eskimo at Barrow than at Anaktuvuk Pass. Among nonnatives, I expected females to prefer traditional home-type environments more than their spouses, for whom the ruggedness and isolation of the Arctic were still major attractions. Thirdly, I expected age differences: adults and older folk would be set in their ways and prefer familiar environments; youngsters, for reasons of age as well as schooling, would be either more variable in their preferences or be attracted by the more exotic environments. Finally, I expected native/nonnative differences, the non-native to prefer the more rugged, and richly vegetated landscapes. And since he was generally unconcerned with subsistence problems, the nonnative would likely prefer the more exotic environments as well. In addition, differences were expected among nonnative populations, based on different occupations and environmental experience. Also, I expected the Delaware group to be much more oriented to a warm environment, and, being more randomly oriented to environment than the rather select group of nonnatives in Alaska, to exhibit more variable preferences, generally.

The test data validated a number of these predictions, though not all of them.

Village differences: Barrow and Anaktuvuk Pass groups differed significantly on topography and water, Barrowites preferring landscapes with less rugged relief and more water. However, the Wainwright population, though intermediate in water preferences, ranked even lower on topography than Barrow, and was also lowest on the vegetation dimension.[8]

The higher ranking of Barrow on topography may be related to the larger number of youngsters included in the Barrow sample, as well as to the inland origin of a good number of Barrow residents. The lower ranking of Wainwright on vegetation may relate to the fact that at the time of testing, it was the best supplied of the three Eskimo villages with fuel, a locally available low-grade coal.

Anaktuvuk Pass groups, occupying the highest of the Eskimo villages studied, and the poorest in fuel sources as well as the closest to the treeline, ranked highest on topography and vegetation. On temperature, Barrow ranked highest and Anaktuvuk Pass lowest, a range consistent with both geography and degree of acculturation.

---

[8] High rankings signify, according to dimension, preference for slides showing more rugged relief features, more richly or densely vegetated areas, landscapes obviously better-supplied with water, and warmer environments. Low rankings indicate, by contrast, preference for less rugged relief, less dense vegetation (e.g. grass rather than forest), less watered landscapes, and cooler environments.

Sex differences: Males and females of all major groups varied similarly on the four dimensions: males tended to prefer landscapes with rougher topography and with indications of water, while females preferred more richly vegetated landscapes and warmer environments. Greatest score discrepancies between male and female had been expected for the most acculturated groups, but, in fact, the greatest difference was that between males and females of Anaktuvuk Pass, the most traditional Eskimo group. Anaktuvuk males and females, however, were consistent in their environmental preferences: among Eskimo, they both ranked first (highest) in their preferences for rougher topography, and last (lowest) on the water and temperature dimensions. Interestingly, nonnative males and females ranked even higher on the topography dimension than the Anaktuvuk groups, and lower than the Barrow males and females on temperature, suggesting, oddly enough, a greater preference of the nonnative group for cold environments. Or perhaps this is not so odd, if one considers that the nonnatives are voluntary residents in the Arctic, and remembers the efficiency of their heating technology.

Nonnative sex differences otherwise were consistent with those of the native populations, though the males did not differ significantly from the females on any of the four dimensions analyzed. Male/female differences generally seemed less pronounced among nonnative groups than among native groups, an indication of the clearer sex role differentiation that exists among the latter.

Age differences: Preferences of the different age groups were only in part significant. Temperature rankings, for which one might have expected a major age distinction on physiological grounds, did not clearly vary within any population. There were major differences in the Barrow population, where younger age groups ranked significantly higher on topography, water, and vegetation dimensions, and somewhat lower on temperature, than older age groups. At Anaktuvuk Pass, the youngest age group scored lower than older groups on topography, water, and vegetation, reversing the Barrow rank order. Comparing groups across villages, the Barrow youngsters ranked higher than the youngest Anaktuvuk Pass group on all dimensions, while the oldest group at Anaktuvuk Pass ranked higher than the oldest group at Barrow on all dimensions except temperature. The youngest Barrow group and the oldest Anaktuvuk Pass group seem to represent native extremes, as indeed they may be: the one the most exposed to Western cultural influences, the other the most traditional of the Eskimo groups studied.

Native/nonnative distinctions: These were generally as predicted, nonnatives ranking consistently and significantly higher than natives on the topography and vegetation dimensions. Nonnatives also ranked slightly higher on the water and slightly lower on the temperature dimensions, the last suggesting an unexpected preference for, or tolerance of, cooler environments.

There were also differences among nonnative groups. The Army Special Forces sample ranked highest among nonnative males on topography and water dimensions, and next to lowest on temperature (despite their recent arrival from the southeastern United States, and despite prior training which had emphasized the tropics). Male teachers ranked lowest on the temperature scale, and next to highest on topography and water scales. Female teachers ranked highest of all nonnative groups on the vegetation dimension, and next to highest on the temperature dimension, suggesting a lesser degree of contentment among them than among their spouses.

The most "different" nonnatives were the DEW-line personnel. This group ranked highest of all Alaskan groups tested on the temperature dimension, and lowest of the nonnatives on topography and water. On the vegetation dimension, they ranked highest after the Special Forces group. The preferences of ARL (Arctic Research Laboratory) personnel were, taken as a whole, the closest of nonnative male groups to the native.

Length of Arctic experience apparently had an impact for men different from what it had for women. The shortest-term males ranked somewhat higher on topography, water, and vegetation, and slightly lower on temperature, than those with over two years in the Arctic. Among females, the differences were reversed; those with longer experience of the Arctic ranked higher on topography, water, and vegetation dimensions, and lower on temperature, than females with less Arctic experience. One cannot easily distinguish between what may be in the one case an effect of environmental adaptation over time, and in the other case, an indication of the kind of individual who remains for long periods of time.

The University of Delaware sample ranked significantly lower on topography, and significantly higher on vegetation and temperature dimensions than Arctic nonnatives, though the males of both environments differed more than did the females in their preferences.

To appraise these nonnative data briefly, preferences for landscapes with the more rugged topography and the richer vegetation would appear to indicate a low level of adaptation to the Arctic, which in northern Alaska is a monotony of low relief and tundra vegetation. Yet, nonnative groups in Alaska also ranked low on temperature, which would indicate a preference (or at least tolerance) for cold environments. Actually, while high ranking on vegetation was associated with high topography and low temperature rankings for some, for others a high vegetation ranking was associated with low topography and high temperature rankings. This suggests temperature and topography as the major variables for nonatives. Thus, though all ranked rather high on vegetation, the Special Forces group and male teachers also ranked among the highest on topography and among the lowest on temperature; by contrast, the female teachers, DEW-line personnel and Delaware populations all ranked relatively lower on topography, and ranked among the highest on temperature. This suggests that among nonnatives voluntarily in the Arctic for an extended period, the male teachers were the most contented living under the ruggedly cold environment, at least in terms of their landscape preferences. Their preferences for rough topography, contrasting as this does with Barrow topography, may represent either a distinctive personality characteristic, a preference for the rugged or challenging environment, or a reaction against the dreariness of the north Alaskan Arctic, or both. The one may help explain why the teachers volunteered for Arctic service, but the other--if it applies--may be prognostic of a limited stay for the teachers, depending on the extent to which other variables, environmental and social, are able to reinforce or detract from their perception of the Arctic as a challenging environment.

At the other extreme, the scores of the DEW-line personnel--among the highest on vegetation, and the highest on temperature--indicate a lower level of contentment with the Arctic environment. This suggests the importance of high salaries for retaining the nonnative technicians in the Arctic, who lack the kinds of motivation-- environmental, scientific, and social--that apparently do attract such groups as teachers, scientists, and missionaries. The low ranking of DEW-line personnel on topography, below that of other nonnatives in the Arctic, and below Delaware student populations as well, suggests as much a personality-related preference as an adaptation to the low-lying Arctic coastal plain.

As a final consideration, previous environmental experience seemed also to affect responses. Arctic natives who had been away from the Arctic ranked significantly higher on topography, water, and vegetation dimensions, and lower on the temperature dimension, than those who had never left the Arctic. Since the group with non-Arctic experience generally excludes the school age groups, the fact of these differences, in the same direction as those which distinguish between younger and older age groups (as well as between native and nonnative groups), would appear yet more significant. Among non-Eskimo groups, both Arctic and non-Arctic, those who had previously lived in areas of Mediterranean-type climate (Cs in the Koppen classification)

anked highest on the topography dimension, while those from the humid tropics
Köppen type A) ranked lowest. Those with steppe (BS) climate experience ranked low-
st on the water dimension (there were none with desert experience). On other scales,
onnative Arctic and Delaware populations diverged; among the former, for example,
nose with steppe backgrounds ranked highest on the vegetation dimension, while the
teppe-exposed Delaware group ranked lowest on that scale. Similarly, those with
ropical experience among Arctic populations ranked high on temperature while the
»elaware population with tropical experience ranked among the lowest on the tempera-
ure scale.

These rankings appear, on the whole, remarkably consistent with the adaptation
evel concepts discussed above, relating to the significance of the interaction of current
nd past environmental experiences on environmental attitudes and perceptions.

Most of the landscape choices of both natives and nonnatives can be placed
vithin certain basic categories of response. Many exhibited preferences for home-type
nvironments, either because they genuinely liked such environments, or because of
ncertainty concerning the unknown alternative. Others preferred landscapes character-
zed by features deficient in the local environment, the lack of which made life difficult
r less comfortable. An alien population in an Arctic coastal plain chose slides depict-
ng forests and mountains, features more familiar to them. A native population short of
uel preferred slides showing scattered trees, for their presumed fuel potential.
:hoices often indicate not only what is attractive in landscape, but what appears defici-
nt in the local or home environment.

Other choices depend on acculturation level. Subsistence-oriented Eskimo
hoose environments similar to their native areas. As they become involved in wage
abor, travel, see movies, come into contact with and are influenced by alien populations,
heir landscape preferences change. Non-subsistence features become more interesting
nd attractive. A number of Eskimo expressed a preference for a coastal resort scene
ver that of an Arctic environment which had more obvious subsistence value. Similarly,
he choices of nonnatives become more consistent with those of natives as the local
nvironment takes on more meaning for them.

There are also preferences for the exotic, the alien, the landscape which
ppears attractive simply because it is different. Youngsters, field scientists, and
onnatives generally, who are free from subsistence concerns, expectably make such
hoices. Other preferences emerge: for open or closed environments; for rugged or
gentle relief features; for arid or humid conditions; for the landscape explicitly endowed

with water. Here, culture, personality, and sex variables all operate.[9]

As a measure of environmental adaptation, one could relate landscape preferences to the nature of the environment occupied by the respondent or his group. Divergence between one's ideal and actual worlds would indicate level of adaptation to, or contentment with, one's own environment. But this might as reasonably be considered a scale or measure of "environmental curiosity." In reality, no simple connection between any such measure and nonnative adaptability to any environment is to be expected, given the significance of previous environmental experience on adaptation level, and thus on the meaning of the individual's responses; and given, too, the significance of motivation as a major determinant of individual and group effectiveness in any environment.

The interpretation of adaptation level from data on environmental attitudes has just begun. Combined test results should provide a measure of the consistency of individual and group responses. Deeper probing into photo-slide test results is also in order. Not only is further analysis of landscape preferences required, relating to the strength of individual and group preferences for certain landscape features when other features are controlled, but even more basic questions are at issue. To what extent are environments depicted by photo-slides perceived as equivalent to real environments? What really is seen in the color photograph? What visual cues provide the evidence for such conditions as temperature, humidity, and, even more basically, habitability?

These efforts to probe variability in environmental perception and behavior ar thus far exploratory. Environmental perceptions do vary; but the variability that characterizes different populations is predictable only to the extent that the major variables of environmental perception and response are understood. These must include, in addition to the consideration of environment, a consideration of the complex human organism, to include physiology, cultural heritage, experience, and personality in both their universal and unique dimensions. No one can know everything environmentally significant about everyone in every population or culture group. But we need

---

[9]Robert Beck, a psychologist at N.Y.U., has suggested that his own and other studies indicate that females should rank higher than males on the water dimension. This is corroborated to a certain extent among the Delaware populations sampled, but not among Arctic nonnative populations, and not among any of the native populations. Similarly, among the Delaware population, males ranked higher than females on the vegetation and temperature dimensions, but the opposite is the case for Arctic nonnative and Eskimo populations with the exception of DEW-line personnel, who were also an exception in their low ranking on the water dimension.

to know more than culture history, economy, society, and policy to understand the variable success of individuals and populations in adapting to environment.

The need to know exists; the means for knowing also exists, in the wealth of concepts and research techniques now available from the behavioral sciences. The era of environmentalism witnessed an early attempt by geographers to function as behavioral scientists. Though a strong reaction was necessary in order to re-emphasize the significance of culture in accounting for mankind's variable relationships with, and achievements in, environment, the anti-environmentalist legacy of that era has discouraged the study of man's environmental sensitivities and behaviors. Without question, this has been a loss to geography; it may well have been a loss to behavioral science as well.

APPENDIX

Samples from the Photo-slide Test

SAMPLES FROM THE PHOTO-SLIDE TEST

The photo-slide test consisted of color slides of various landforms projected simultaneously in pairs. Some of the pairs used have been reproduced here in black and white.

The designation "native" refers to Eskimo populations in Arctic Alaska, while the designation "nonnative" refers to the non-Eskimo populations in the same areas of Arctic Alaska. All other non-Eskimo populations are specified: e.g., "University of Delaware males," "Newark Junior High School females," etc. Village designations-- "Barrow," "Wainwright," and "Anaktuvuk Pass"--refer to native populations only in those villages.

Populations are placed, for the most part, beneath the landscape they preferred when shown each pair. A "(-)" alongside a population indicates that the population had fewer individuals choosing the landscape under which it is listed than chose the other slide; the reason for its being placed on the side of the weaker preference is that the population it was compared with had significantly greater preference for the other slide.

Significance levels were determined using the Chi Square test, with Yates' correction.

Wainwright	.02	Anaktuvuk Pass	(-)
Barrow	.001	Anaktuvuk Pass	(-)
Native female	.01	Native male	(-)
Native under 19	.02	Native over 19	(-)

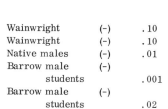

Wainwright	(-)	.10	Barrow	
Wainwright	(-)	.10	Anaktuvuk Pass	
Native males	(-)	.01	Nonnative males (Arctic)	
Barrow male	(-)		Barrow female	
students		.001	students	
Barrow male	(-)		Newark Jr. H. S. male	
students		.02		students

Barrow   (-)   . 10   Anaktuvuk Pass
Wainwright   . 005   Barrow
Barrow female   (-)   . 10   Newark Jr. H. S.
    students   females

Under 19 (native)   . 01   Over 19 (native)
Nonnative males   Native males
    (Arctic)   . 01   Barrow male
Newark Jr. H. S. males   . 001   students   (-)
Newark Jr. H. S. males   . 10   Neward Jr. H. S.   (-)
Univ. of Del. females   . 02   females
                                       Nonnative Arctic females (-)

Nonnative (Arctic)	.001	Native	
Native under 19 (-)	.05	Native over 19	
Newark Jr. H. S. males	.10	Barrow male students	(-)
Newark Jr. H. S. females	.005	Barrow female students	
Univ. of Dela. females	.10	Univ. of Dela. males	(-)

Anaktuvuk Pass	.001	Barrow
Newark Jr. H. S. males	.001	Barrow male students
Newark Jr. H. S. females	.05	Barrow female students
Univ. of Dela. males	.05	Nonnative Arctic males
Native females over 19	.05	Nonnative females over 19

Native males	.001
Natives under 19	.05
Native males	.10

Nonnative males (Arctic)
Natives over 19 (-)
Native females

Wainwright	.10
Barrow	.02
University of Delaware males	.02
Wainwright	.001
Univ. of Dela. females	.10
Native over 19	.10

Barrow (-)
Anaktuvuk Pass
Nonnative Arctic males (-)

Anaktuvuk Pass (-)
Nonnative Arctic females (-)
Native under 19 (-)

CHAPTER IV

THE PERCEPTION OF STORM HAZARD ON
THE SHORES OF MEGALOPOLIS

Robert W. Kates

The outer shore of Megalopolis consists of 1300 miles of sand bar, bluff, and tidal marsh. On the twenty percent of this frontage that is developed, air photos reveal over 125,000 man-made structures within ten feet of sea level. The people who live and work in these structures share a common orientation to the ocean, and are in turn subject to a set of natural hazards posed by the onshore movement of wind and water powered by the impressive energy of atmosphere and ocean.

The degree to which these hazards are recognized by those who locate adjacent to the shore is the subject of this paper. It is part of a long-term inquiry into the relation between man and the more hazardous aspects of the natural environment.[1] But it arises also from a pragmatic concern with the rising toll of storm damages and with subsequent public pressure for increased protection, relief, and insurance against wave and associated wind damage.[2] And this research report is part of a larger study aimed specifically at understanding the processes of growth and development in areas subject to coastal inundation and within easy reach of Megalopolitan population centers.[3]

---

[1] The most recent general statement is in Ian Burton and Robert W. Kates "Perception of Natural Hazards in Resource Management," Natural Resources Journal, III (1964), pp. 412-441.

[2] Ian Burton and Robert W. Kates, "The Flood Plain and the Seashore: A Comparative Analysis of Hazard Zone Occupance," Geographical Review, LIV (1964), p. 366.

[3] Ian Burton, Robert W. Kates, John R. Mather, and Rodman E. Snead, The Shores of Megalopolis: Coastal Occupance and Human Adjustment to Flood Hazard, Publications in Climatology, XVII, No. 3 (Elmer, New Jersey: C.W. Thornthwaite Associates, 1965). Pp. 435-603.

Fifteen sites along the coast from North Carolina to New Hampshire were chosen for intensive study (Figure IV-1). These sites are diverse in settlement, in regional location, and in subjection to natural hazard. They include urbanized areas with a coastal orientation, small settlements and fishing ports, seasonally occupied recreational areas, and coastal areas devoid of permanent human occupance.

At each site, excluding the empty shore, a non-random sample of permanent residents, seasonal home owners, and commercial managers was selected for interviews; in all, 371 usable interviews were obtained. All respondents were potentially subject to some hazard of tidal inundation from coastal storms, but fifteen percent had ground-floor elevations higher than the previously recorded maxima of flooding. In content, the interviews were designed to explore existing hypotheses of human adjustment to natural hazard and to delineate individual hazard perceptions.[4]

Our present understanding of human adjustment to hazardous natural environments has been derived mainly from flood plains, but these observations are reinforced by other research, notably that of anthropologists.[5] Their studies suggest that adjustments to natural hazards are common in most societies and at all levels of technological skill. However, the level of adjustment is often sub-optimal--that is, fewer and weaker steps are taken than are required to minimize the effects of the natural hazard, while permitting maximum use of resources associated with that hazard.

The causes of sub-optimal behavior are complex and manifold. Natural hazards include a variety of extreme or rare geophysical events. They are not easily amenable to the prevailing calculus of risk based on relative frequency, and it is difficult, even with technical-scientific expertise, to specify an optimal set of adjustments. Even were such specifications theoretically feasible, to make use of them would require a range of information beyond the capacity of the ordinary individual residing or working within a hazard area. Finally, the pattern of decision-making that leads to sub-optimal choice seems to be inherent in the human condition.

We are, in Simon's terms, either satisficers, content with sub-optimal solutions, or, as the traditionalists suggest, born optimizers, saddled with ignorance and

---

[4] The portion of the interview schedule dealing with tidal flood hazard is reproduced as Appendix: "Tidal Flood Hazard Questionnaire."

[5] See Burton and Kates, "Perception of Natural Hazards in Resource Management, for a summary of some relevant studies.

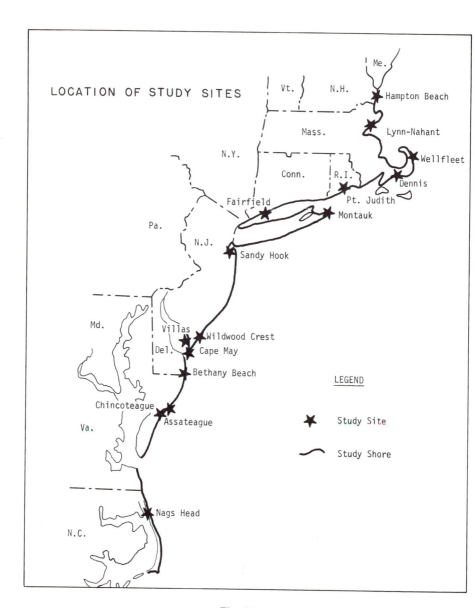

Fig. IV-1

ill fortune.[6] We aspire to, but never reach, the ideal response. A choice between these models of man may always elude us, but we can at least study how men elect to order their uncertain environments. Ignorance and ill fortune can be operationally defined in terms of individual experience of hazard, and the extent of damage suffered. We can inquire what men do or would do about hazard and compare their responses with some technical standard of what men could do. We can compare variations in behavior and perception between areas of different magnitudes of hazard and uncertainty, and between natural hazards of different types. Our coastal data illustrate one such set of relations--that between past and present storm experience and anticipations of the future course of events.

This relation is fundamental to the study of decision-making. In technical terms, future expectation is the specification of a set of outcomes. Based on these perceived sets of outcomes, actions may or may not be taken to reduce damage. How are these outcomes formulated, on what are they based, and whence do they derive?

The specification of storm hazard cannot come solely from scientific and technical knowledge. Even in this area we are woefully inadequate. Climatology, meteorology, oceanography, and coastal geomorphology all seek to define significant elements of the land-sea interface. There is no shortage of description, but meaningful measurements--meaningful in terms of human occupance--are lacking.

We can be certain that major damage-causing storms will affect the area under study in the future. But we cannot state with precision the type of storm to be feared, the frequency of its recurrence, the degree of its magnitude, the likely area of run-up. We can record the past experience of others, but despite the long familiarity of man and sea, our information is rudimentary. The most destructive storm of the recent past, that of March 6-7, 1962, was born off Florida, passed northward to devastate the mid-Atlantic coast over a fetch of upwards of a thousand miles--and then, without warning, under clear skies and with a calm sea, sent swells a thousand miles south to batter the Florida coast again.[7]

---

[6]H.A. Simon, Models of Man: Social and Rational (New York: John Wiley, 1957). For a discussion of decision-making models, see Robert W. Kates, Hazard and Choice Perception in Flood Plain Management, Department of Geography Research Paper No. 78, University of Chicago (Chicago: University of Chicago Press, 1962), pp. 12-28.

[7]U.S. House of Representatives, Improvement of Storm Forecasting Procedures, Hearing before the Subcommittee on Oceanography of the Committee on Merchant and Marine Fisheries, 87th Cong., 2nd Sess., April 4, 1962.

Or consider frequency. A Laboratory of Climatology survey has identified classes of storms significant for human occupance from 1935-64 by twenty-five-mile sectors from 1935 to 1964. Over our study area, there averaged three storms per twenty-five miles in the first decade, six storms in the second decade, and seventeen in the third decade.[8] Has there been a phenomenal rise in storm occurrence, or is the increase the result of improved reporting of storms, or of more intensive occupance of low-lying areas--lending new significance to storms that would earlier have passed unnoticed?

It is against this background of the common occurrence of coastal storms, combined with great temporal and spatial uncertainty about their specific characteristics, that the knowledge and experience of residents should be viewed.

Almost all our respondents had some knowledge of storm hazard. (Table IV-1). Only three evinced ignorance that storms occur along their stretch of coast. Two-thirds of our respondents recalled being aware of the hazard when they first settled there, and ninety percent had experienced a storm during their period of occupance. Fifty percent had suffered some water damage and many more had suffered wind damage. Conscious perception of at least some degree of natural hazard is generally more widespread than popular accounts suggest, but an exceptionally high proportion of coastal dwellers display such awareness. Comparable studies on riverine flood plains reveal far less knowledge of hazard.

This reflects the distinctive locational orientation of our coastal respondents. In contrast to flood-plain dwellers and to inhabitants of zones of high seismic activity, for example, coast dwellers do not just happen to be where they are. It is the adjacent sea that attracted them to their location, as over half of them suggested in response to an open-ended question. The coastal dweller, attracted to the sea for recreation or commerce, becomes keenly aware of its varied states. Even the seasonal visitor, who usually sees the sea only in its more placid moods, seems to share this heightened awareness. On the coast, the daily variation of tide reminds us of the sea's potential for changing its level. And the use of boats, beaches, and water sports, with their sensitivity to weather, provides additional familiarity with phenomena and so contributes to this awareness.

But this appreciation of the force of storm and tide does not carry over into a realistic assessment of the future. As Table IV-2 shows, despite the fact that ninety

---

[8] Burton et al., The Shores of Megalopolis, pp. 546-549.

TABLE IV-1

INFORMATION AND FUTURE EXPECTATIONS OF COASTAL RESPONDENTS

Present Hazard Information	Expectation of Future Hazards (% of respondents)				Total
	No storms or damage expected	Storms and damage uncertain	Storms expected but no or uncertain damage	Storms and damage expected	
No knowledge	0.8	-	-	-	0.8
Knowledge	2.2	2.4	4.3	0.8	9.7
One experience	6.5	5.7	8.4	9.4	30.0
Two or more experiences	4.6	8.7	22.7	23.0	59.0
Total	14.1	16.8	35.4	33.2	99.5
(Number of Respondents)	(52)	(62)	(131)	(123)	(368)

percent of our respondents experienced storms, only two-thirds expect storms in the future. And although half of them suffered some damage in the past, only a third expect a future storm to entail damage for themselves.

Expectations of future outcomes cannot be understood on the basis of simple awareness of the past; such expectations arise out of a process called interpretation. Our knowledge and experience of real events in the world is personalized and distorted by preconceived concepts of uniqueness and repetitiveness. These concepts are presented in Table IV-2, which classifies respondents on the basis of their replies to structured and unstructured questions about storms. From these verbal clues, we somewhat subjectively derive our categories of interpretation.

Most respondents interpret storms as repetitive events, and many of them feel that the repetition is in some fashion constant: "Just the process of nature in this area for storms to come every year"; "We get storms, with serious ones at about ten year intervals." For others, storms are increasing, owing either to the action of man-- "They are shooting those rockets up on Wallop's Island"--or to a perceived migration of hurricane tracks--"They are running up the coast." The spatial pattern may be reversed; some perceive it as "the cycle goes from North Carolina to Florida." These respondents

TABLE IV-2

INTERPRETATION AND FUTURE EXPECTATIONS OF
COASTAL RESPONDENTS

Present Interpretation of Hazards	Expectation of Future Hazards (% of respondents)				Total
	No storms or damage expected	Storms and damage uncertain	Storms expected but no or uncertain damage	Storms and damage expected	
I Respondents do not share in the common knowledge of storms	0.9	-	-	-	0.9
II Respondents share in the common knowledge of storms but:					
a) Deny the common image of storms	2.1	0.3	0.6	0.3	3.3
b) Think storms are unique	5.3	4.0	-	-	9.8
c) Think storms are repetitive and also think:					
1. They are personally excluded	3.7	0.9	0.3	-	4.9
2. Storms are decreasing in time or space	1.2	-	1.5	0.3	3.0
3. Storm trend can not be ascertained	-	2.7	16.2	12.8	31.7
4. Storms are constant in time or space	0.6	0.9	20.1	21.6	43.2
5. Storms are increasing in time or space	-	-	0.3	2.4	2.7
Total	14.3	8.8	39.0	37.4	99.5
(Number of Respondents)	(47)	(29)	(128)	(123)	(327)

all see storms as decreasing in frequency or intensity.

For a fair number of other respondents, storms are either unique or unknowable: "The 1962 storm was a freak"; "Nature is too unpredictable." And for a very few, hazard is denigrated or even wished away by semantic magic: "We never have any bad storms"; "We might have a couple of hurricanes, but not a storm." The coastal resident who interprets a storm as a freak, unique event, gains no sense of direction from his experience; his future expectations are based on uncertainty and on a desire to deny hazard.

But quite different interpretations of the course of nature may lead to similar expectations. Some respondents who view the repetition of storms as an ordered event derive comfort from their supposed cyclical frequency: "We get storms once in ninety years, we're not due for another." If a major storm occurs and an individual escapes serious damage, the net impact frequently reinforces feelings of security. Storms might be expected in the future, but they will not affect me. Similarly, elderly retired couples, although aware of storm hazard, may feel secure from them. Storms seem to them to be spaced far enough apart to assure them of security during their few remaining years.

These interpretations, garnered from the spoken clues of the world inside peoples' heads, help to explain the gap between actual experience and future expectation. They help to answer the puzzling question as to why people continue to place themselves in areas of high natural hazard. They show how common experiences are individually interpreted so as to enhance the security of expectations. They suggest something of the way men think about natural phenomena.

Most hazards are apparently random phenomena. Members of the technical-scientific community have by training been prepared to accept a high degree of uncertainty in their scientific work, if not in their private lives. They strive to order the unknowns of natural phenomena, but are prepared to accept the unexplained and to await tomorrow's knowledge.

Our respondents, intelligent and articulate lay people, react to uncertainty in a fundamentally different way. They react to the random occurrence of storms by making events knowable, finding order where none exists, identifying cycles on the basis of the sketchiest of knowledge or folk insight, and, in general, striving to reduce the uncertainty of the threat of hazard. Or conversely, they deny all knowability, resign themselves to the uniqueness of natural phenomena, throw up their hands in impotent despair and assign their fates to a higher power.

Each of these types of explanation has its exponents, but seventy-five percent of the responses of coastal residents fall in one of two categories of interpretation. We had expected to find that the less a hazard was understood, the greater would be the range of interpretations, and that where common knowledge was ambiguous or obscure, the distortion of that knowledge--measured by the variance of interpretation--would increase. Evidence from flood plains suggested that variations of all sorts--in experience, in interpretation, in future flood expectations, and in the perception and adoption of hazard-reducing actions--were greatest where floods occurred often enough to be common but not so often as to make their occurrence certain.[9] The range of individual perceptions fell off in areas of frequent floods or very infrequent floods, where the absence or the occurrence of events seemed immediately and overwhelmingly explicable.

The coastal data reinforce this notion. The left sides of Figure IV-2 show the range of response to four kinds of questions asked in 216 interviews of flood plain dwellers resident where floods occurred on an average of four in every ten years.[10] The right sides show the responses of 371 coastal residents where damage-producing storms occurred on an average of nine in every ten years. By comparison with the flood plain dwellers, range of response among coastal residents is narrow on all counts.

Space does not permit a discussion of how the perception of hazard is translated into behavior designed to reduce damage from storms. But the public policy implications of our study are clear and straightforward. With the exception of a few villages inhabited by retired couples or impoverished fishermen, who in any event are well aware of coastal hazard, coastal users are relatively well educated and well-to-do.[11] They have come to the shore to partake of the attractions found at the interface of land and sea or to serve those who are so attracted. They are, by and large, knowing and well-informed about the general nature of the hazard they face; and as to the details, they are little worse off than the technical-scientific community. A high proportion of coastal dwellers take minimal steps to reduce their hazard, but many of them elect to live at considerable risk rather than reduce their seaward amenities by conservation

---

[9] Kates, Hazard and Choice Perception, pp. 83-96.

[10] These data are summarized in Robert W. Kates, "Perceptual Regions and Regional Perception in Flood Plain Management, " Papers and Proceedings of the Regional Science Association, II (1963), p. 220.

[11] Among the respondents, 43 percent had some college education and 22 percent had annual incomes in excess of $15,000. These compare with percentages of 16.5 and 17.2, respectively, for the U.S. population.

measures. Some, for example, have opposed the construction of seawalls; others have knowingly leveled dunes in order to improve views and accessibility to beaches.[12] In such a situation, government action to protect beach-front property could be taken only through considerably extending the concept of the welfare state. However, given the long tradition of policy-by-crisis in resource management,[13] it is quite conceivable that some such development and commitment might occur, owing to the pressures, human and natural, that the shores of Megalopolis inevitably face. A more desirable alternative would be an increased effort by government to improve scientific understanding of physical processes, to share such knowledge with the users of the shore, and to encourage patterns of land use that minimize damage.

On the facade of the University of Wyoming is emblazoned the slogan, "Strive, the Conquest of Nature is Won--Not Given". The awesome power of the sea leads to the reflection that the conquest of nature is neither won nor given except in the minds of men.

---

[12] Fairfield, Connecticut, the North Shore of Long Island, and Narragansett Bay Rhode Island, provide instances of such anti-conservation action.

[13] The basic statement on the relation between crisis and flood plain management is in Henry C. Hart, "Crisis, Community, and Consent in Water Politics," Law and Contemporary Problems, XXII (1957), pp. 510-537.

VARIATION BETWEEN FLOODPLAIN AND COASTAL
RESPONDENTS IN MAJOR HAZARD PARAMETERS

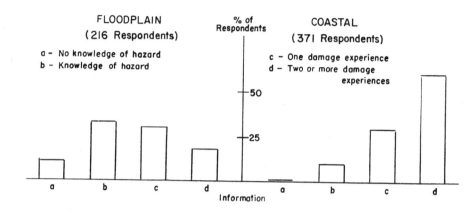

FLOODPLAIN
(216 Respondents)

a - No knowledge of hazard
b - Knowledge of hazard

% of
Respondents

COASTAL
(371 Respondents)

c - One damage experience
d - Two or more damage
    experiences

Information

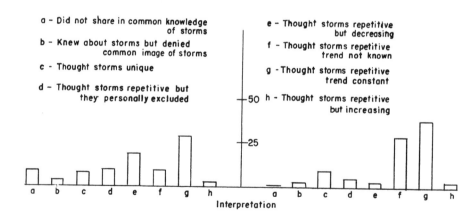

a - Did not share in common knowledge
    of storms
b - Knew about storms but denied
    common image of storms
c - Thought storms unique
d - Thought storms repetitive but
    they personally excluded

e - Thought storms repetitive
    but decreasing
f - Thought storms repetitive
    trend not known
g - Thought storms repetitive
    trend constant
h - Thought storms repetitive
    but increasing

Interpretation

Fig. IV-2

Variation Between Floodplain and Coastal Respondents in Major Hazard Parameters

VARIATION BETWEEN FLOODPLAIN AND COASTAL RESPONDENTS IN MAJOR HAZARD PARAMETERS

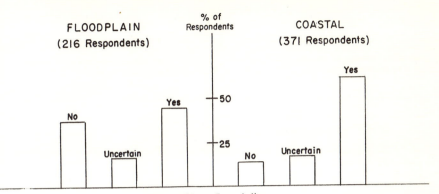

Future Storm Expectation

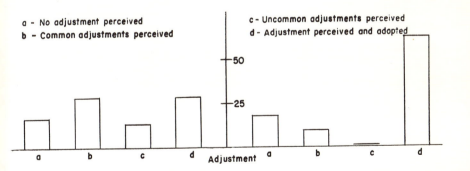

Adjustment

Fig. IV-2 (Cont'd)

Variation Between Floodplain and Coastal Respondents in Major Hazard Parameters

APPENDIX
TIDAL FLOOD HAZARD
QUESTIONNAIRE

SITE NO.

SCHEDULE NO.

F 1. Do you have any bad storms or hurricanes along this part of the coast?

YES   NO   UNCERTAIN   EXPLAIN UNCERTAINTY

_____

_____

_____

_____

_____

IF <u>NO</u>, PASS DIRECTLY TO F 6.

F 2. Have you had any bad storms or hurricanes while you have (been in Business) (lived) here?

YES   NO   UNCERTAIN   EXPLAIN UNCERTAINTY

PROBE: WHEN, YEARS, DESCRIPTION

_____

_____

_____

_____

IF <u>NO</u>, PASS DIRECTLY TO F 4.

F 3. Did you have any damage in the storm of _____ or _____ ?

SPECIFY STORM _____

_____

_____

_____

F 4. Do you know how high the water gets along the shore in the worst storm or hurricane that you know about?

EXACT STATEMENT _____

_____

_____

_____

PROBE IF NECESSARY AND CONVERT TO NEAREST FOOT ABOVE SEA LEVEL

F 5. How about where we are now standing? How high would the water get here?

EXACT STATEMENT _____

_____

_____

_____

PROBE IF NECESSARY AND CONVERT TO NEAREST FOOT ABOVE SEA LEVEL

F 6. Do you think that you will have, or there will be, a bad storm or hurricane while you are (in business) or (living) here?

      YES   NO   UNCERTAIN

PROBE, WHY? _____

_____

_____

_____

IF NO, PASS ON TO F 8.

F 7. Do you think you might suffer damage?

      YES   NO   UNCERTAIN

PROBE, WHY? _____

_____

_____

_____

F 8. Do you know of anything being done to reduce damage from storms or hurricanes?

SEA WALLS _____

GROINS OR JETTIES _____

PROTECTIVE DUNES _____

OTHER _____

IMPROVED WARNING _____

LAND-USE REGULATIONS _____

BUILDING CODES _____

INVESTIGATIONS BY LOCAL OR FEDERAL GOV'T _____

F 9.   Have you ever done anything personally to get action to reduce danger from storms or hurricanes?

      YES   NO   UNCERTAIN

      PROBE: WHAT? _____

F 10.   Do you know of anything that you might do personally with this property or your belongings to reduce damages, either before or during a storm?

      YES   NO   UNCERTAIN

      PROBE: IF RESPONDENT SUGGESTS KNOWLEDGE, PROBE FOR ADOPTION, AND CODE ANSWERS 1 FOR KNOWLEDGE, AND 3 FOR ADOPTION. IF ACTION APPEARS SOLELY DESIGNED FOR WIND ACTION, NOTE THAT AS WELL.

REQUIRING NO PRIOR ACTION: REQUIRING PRIOR ACTION:

      DISCONNECT UTILITIES &   STAND-BY PREPARATIONS _____

      MOTORS _____   _____

      KEEP WATER OUT _____   STRUCTURAL CHANGE _____

      HELP WATER THROUGH _____   ELEVATION & REMOVAL _____

      ELEVATION & REMOVAL _____   REORGANIZATION _____

      _____   DO NOTHING _____

      PERSONAL SAFETY _____

      OTHER _____

F 11.   Did you know anything about the storm problems when you decided to move here?

      YES   NO   UNCERTAIN

      PROBE: IF YES. Did it bother you at the time?

      PROBE: IF NO. Knowing what you now know about storms, would you (move) (start) (locate) here again?

CHAPTER V

THE VIEW FROM THE ROAD[1]

Donald Appleyard, Kevin Lynch, and John R. Myer

This paper deals with the esthetics of urban highways: the way they look to the driver and his passengers, and what this implies for their design. The authors became interested in the subject out of a concern with the visual formlessness of American cities and an intuition that the new expressway might be one of the best means of re-establishing coherence and order on the metropolitan scale. Also, the highway offers a good example of a design issue that is typical of the city: the problem of designing visual sequences for the observer in motion.

Ugly roads are often taken to be a price of civilization, like sewers or police. The boring, chaotic, disoriented landscape, which seems to be the natural habitat for the American automobile, is tolerated with resignation by the highway user. Even those who are alarmed by the ugliness of the roadways emphasize the repression of vice: roads should melt into the landscape; billboards should be controlled; the scars of construction should be disguised by planting. There is little discussion of turning the highway experience to any positive account.

Yet roadwatching can be a delight. There are many journeys that are enjoyable in themselves: walking, horse-back riding, boating, rides in amusement parks, or on open bus tops. There are even a few roads in this country on which driving a car is a pleasure.

In an affluent society it is possible to choose to build roads in which motion,

---

[1]This paper, which incorporates the substance of Kevin Lynch's presentation at the A. A. G. symposium on Environmental Perception and Behavior, is extracted from the book of the same title published by the M. I. T. Press for the M. I. T.-Harvard Joint Center for Urban Studies, Cambridge, Mass., 1964. It was first published in the Highway Research Record, No. 2, "Community Values as Affected by Transportation," Highway Research Board Publication 1065, 1963, pp. 21-30.

space, and view are organized primarily for enjoyment, like a promenade. But on highways whose primary function is the carriage of goods and people, visual form is also of fundamental importance and can be shaped without interfering with traffic flow. It is the landscape seen from these workaday urban highways that will be discussed here from the standpoint of the driver and his passengers; for the purposes of this analysis, the issue of how the highway looks from the outside will be ignored.

The studies were begun by traveling repeatedly along several expressways, particularly the approaches to New York, Hartford, Boston, and Philadelphia. Tape recordings, films, photographs and sketches were used to record everything that the researchers found themselves looking at. Subsequently, an analysis was made of this experience, which was checked by analyzing the reactions of a group of twenty people riding along Route C1 in Boston, and a graphic language developed with which to describe it. Finally, this language was refined by using it in designing two hypothetical freeways. This paper presents some of the most general conclusions, neglecting the supporting data, the illustrative material, and the techniques for analysis and design that were also developed.

The highway experience varies with the user. The tourist sees the landscape with a fresh eye; he attaches relatively few personal meanings to it, but is urgently engaged in orienting himself within it. The commuter, or other habitual user of the road, is more likely to ignore larger landscape features, in favor of activities, new objects, or the moving traffic of the road. The driver must watch the scene constantly; his vision is confined to a narrow forward angle and focuses on the events in the road itself. His passenger is freer to look or not to look, has a wider angle of vision, and is not necessarily concerned with immediate traffic. Both driver and passenger are likely to be an inattentive yet captive audience that cannot avoid remarking, if only sub-consciously, the most dramatic events of a scene that is too mobile and too dangerous to be ignored.

The modern car interposes a filter between the driver and the world he is moving through. Sounds, smells, sensations of touch and weather are all diluted. Vision is framed and limited; the driver is relatively inactive. He has less opportunity to stop, explore, or choose his path than does the man on foot. Only the speed, scale, and grace of his movement can compensate for these limitations.

The highway experience has some further special characteristics. It is usually reversible; people may traverse the road in either direction. In addition, it is serial and overlapping; people enter and leave the highway at intermediate points.

The driving experience can be described as a sequence played to the eyes of a captive, somewhat fearful, but partially inattentive audience, whose vision is filtered and directed forward. It is a sequence that must be long, yet reversible and interruptible.

The surveys tended to confirm the obvious regarding the identifiable objects or elements of attention. Along two routes, between one-half and two-thirds of all front-seat sightings were straight ahead. Along another route, two-thirds of these impressions were caused by the near, apparently "moving" objects, rather than the far, seemingly "stable" ones. They included the color and texture of the road surface, objects at the shoulder, signs, guard-rails, retaining walls, etc. Even in periods of wide scanning, attention regularly returns to the road itself. It is concentrated particularly on the foreground at points of decision, or in sharply constricted spaces. But after such experiences the larger landscape is scanned with a fresh eye. This is a moment for visual revelations, when one is sure of an audience attentive to large effect.

Beyond this concentration on near detail, the fundamental sensation of the road, continuously referred to, was the sense of motion and space. This includes the sense of motion of self, the apparent motion of surrounding objects, and the shape of the space being moved through.

The sense of motion of self is perhaps the primary feeling. True kinesthetic sensations are slight in a steadily moving car on a modern highway. The driver receives some cues from his controls, but if the passenger closes his eyes it is very difficult for him to distinguish steadily held turning movements, levels of speed, or even gentle climbs or descents. Bodily sensations become strong only at points of abrupt change in speed or in angle of climb and fall.

Automobile riders depend on vision to give them a sense of the motion they are undergoing. They interpret the apparent motion of surrounding objects that they know to be fixed to be the result of their own progression. These clues may include the passage of roadside detail, the apparent rotation of near objects around far objects, the seeming outward radiation of detail and textures from the point dead ahead, and the illusion of growth as objects approach.

Where surrounding objects are far off, or few, or featureless, or moving with the vehicle, then the sensation is one of floating, of no forward movement. This can be temporarily a pleasant relief, but the inability to reach any goal can soon lead to boredom. Objects might, in such a case, be placed alongside the road, just to reassure the driver about his real motion.

The sense of varied motion is inherently enjoyable if continuous and not too violent. The rhythmical humping of the turnpike across the New Jersey flats, or the sweeping turns of the approach to Boston over the Mystic River Bridge possess such a quality.

The road alignment generates the motion of the driver. Because it predicts future movement, the shape of that line is always of compelling interest. In previous highway studies, this perspective view of the alignment has been considered paramount, along with landscaping and control of roadside detail. The "flowing" line now generally preferred is one sound technique for gaining a harmonious effect. But it is a technique rather than a principle. A kink, a sudden shearing off, a long straight slash may sometimes be part of the artistic content.

The apparent motion of objects can become a delight in itself. The welling up, splitting apart, and falling away of objects can become intricate dances when groups are seen together on a road of complex alignment. Landmarks may move across a background, rotate one way, then another, disappear and reappear, coincide or disperse. The road itself may feint, jog, swerve, or slide past them.

The distant view down the axis of a road, on which the driver can fix his attention without losing touch with his path, is a static experience. If the road is also sloping down at this point, it may be possible to present a view that is meant to be looked at carefully, and that in some way epitomizes the city or an important part of it. Such classical views as San Francisco across the Bay, or New York across the Hudson, are important experiences. Occasionally, when the road makes a sweeping turn or the view is very restricted, the visual field becomes a dynamic one, rotating, rushing, or growing. This is a powerful if unsettling effect.

Things in the landscape that are also in motion, together with their paths of movement, exert a corresponding fascination. The driver will compare his own trajectory with that of a distant train, the ascent of an airplane, the progress of a ship; or relate his path to railroad lines, canals, and other roads which may parallel, interlock, intersect, pass over or under his own. Most impressive of all is the movement of accompanying traffic, which may be the principal visual impression for a commuter.

Simultaneously with the appreciation of objects in motion, there occurs the sense of space, which is basically one of confinement and of the dimensions of that confinement. The space may vary proportionately, through the character of defining walls, objects in the space, or by the position of the observer in that space. The driver can be low down in a concave space, high up in a convex space. The space may be narrow or wide, the walls solid, transparent, netted, smooth or jagged, filled with traffic or deserted.

In sequence, there can be dramatic contrasts between confinement and spatial freedom, such as the entry into Hartford from the Wilbur Cross Parkway, where the road descends towards the city, sinks into a cut, passes through a short tunnel, and bursts out into the central park.

One of the most important visual sensations is the relation of scale between a large environment and the observer, a feeling of adequacy when confronted with a vast space. The automobile with its speed and personal control begins to reduce the disparity in scale between man and the city, allowing man again to feel powerful and big enough to relate to his environment. The design of the vehicle as an extension of man, therefore, becomes a critical factor in his experience.

At the next level of organization, the driver is engaged in orienting himself to the environment, in building up some image of it. Movement along the road consists of a succession of approaches to goals, which may be prominent landmarks, focal points, or other paths to be attained. By them he measures his progress and foretells his future. They may be distant goals that symbolize his final destination, or they may be nearer objects that divide the road into visual segments.

Goals may be organized in succession, as on the prairie when one proceeds from silo to silo. They may overlap, or there may be one dominant goal constantly visible, with minor goals playing against it. Thus the towers of Manhattan indicate the eventual destination of the New Jersey Turnpike while it maneuvers through the monumental landscape peopled by oil refineries, the Newark Airport, and the Pulaski Skyway.

Beyond the sense of progression from goal to goal, one is concerned with orientation in the general environment, with locating its principal features and relating oneself to them. This is partly a practical, partly an esthetic activity. A clear image of the city structure is a necessary counterpart for driver orientation on the urban freeway. Reliance on signs is not enough. There is positive pleasure in being able to recognize the urban scene and fit it together.

The shapelessness of Boston from the Mystic Bridge approach, and the frequent periods of orientation blindness are disappointing and disquieting, whereas the edge of Manhattan, from either the East or West River Drives, is satisfying just because the relationship between city and water is made visible.

The image of the highway itself may also be clarified. Successive sections may be visibly differentiated so that they can be recognized as distinct parts. Thus the motorist can see that he is "in the hilly part" as well as "approaching the center." The general alignment may be made to appear as a simple geometric form. Continuities of edge, surface, or rhythm may be used. Typical sequences and gradients may be developed, and the sequence in one direction may be made recognizably different from the sequence in the other. The road ahead may be exposed and strategic points may be articulated. The form of interchanges may be clarified, so that driving decisions become self-evident and the shape is congruent with the principal flow of traffic.

Finally, the driver seeks meaning in his environment. He relates the visible objects to the stock of ideas in his mind. Such visual clues as the sight of an activity are essential to comprehension of the city. When the road makes apparently purposeless movements, or when a lively center of activity like Boston's food market is hidden from the road that passes overhead, an opportunity for contributing to an expressive environment is lost. Current efforts to "buffer" fast roads from the city by depression, distance, or landscaping are reducing the road experience to dull meaninglessness.

Would it be possible to use the highway as a means of education, a way of making the rider aware of the functioning, history, and human values of his world? The highway could become a sequential exposition of the city, by visually relating it to focal points, and picking out symbolic and historical landmarks. Travel guides, tape recordings, and signs, if imaginatively executed, could point out the meaning of the scene.

The most powerful experiences occur when space, motion, orientation, and meaning reinforce each other--when a landmark that is rooted in community history is the visible goal of a journey and the visible pivot about which the road turns. The pivot of motion on a highway today is all too likely a temporary shanty, and its goal a whiskey advertisement.

Using all these elements, the basic artistic problem of the highway is the shaping of its sequential form. In such form the principal aim is to preserve continuity while developing, embellishing, and contrasting the material. The road itself furnishes an essential thread of continuity, but it must be supported by successions of space, motion, orientation, and meaning which become parts of a connected whole. An overlapping of goals may do this, the repetition of previous movements, or a basic rhythm of attention.

The tempo of attention appears to be a sensitive index of the quality of a road. Where this tempo is rapid, attention concentrates on near objects straight ahead on the road; where the tempo is slow, scanning takes place. When either of these is prolonged, a sense of oppression or boredom occurs. Perhaps there is an optimum range for this time interval between strong impressions. Were this true, the roadscape should possess a basic, though varying, beat.

The traditional sequential form is to set in motion a drive toward a final goal. This drive may be interrupted, prolonged, and embellished at rhythmic intervals, but it never entirely loses forward momentum, and it achieves its destination at a climax, subsiding then to a conclusion with tension resolved. This is a useful model for highway design but it suffers from the handicap that the audience enters and leaves at different points. Thus, sequential form may have to be more like a magazine serial, with self-contained episodes, or it may have to be symmetrical with climaxes at both ends for a two-way audience, or the unified climactic form may have to be abandoned for the articulated but "endless" composition of the kind typified in jazz.

The principal objectives in shaping the highway visual experience may now be summarized. The first is to present the viewer with a rich, coherent sequential form, a form that has continuity, rhythm, and development, and that provides contrasts, well-joined transitions, and a moving balance.

The second objective is to clarify and strengthen the drivers' image of the environment, to give him a picture that is well-structured, distinct, and as far-ranging as possible. He should be able to locate himself, the road, and the major features of the landscape, to recognize those features with surety, and to sense how he is moving by or approaching them.

The third objective is to deepen the observer's grasp of the meaning of his environment--to give him an understanding of the use, history, nature, or symbolism of the highway and its surrounding landscape. The roadside should be a fascinating book to read on the run. Ideally, all three objectives should be achieved by means that interlock at every level.

These analyses are still fragmentary. It would be useful to study further the experience of the commuter, the problems of transition, the design of terminals, and the view of the highway from outside. Neither the design of highway networks nor the whole system of movement in the city has been considered. Both await the efforts of future research.

To illustrate some of the implications of the study, Figures 1 through 5 show a hypothetical design for Boston's inner belt expressway. Current plans locate this route in a loose and shapeless ring about the downtown, often too far out and suppressed to maintain orientation or visual contact with the center, and connected only sporadically to the incoming radials.

The redesigned road sets out to clarify three aspects of the environment for the road user: (a) the natural features (in this case, the harbor, rivers, and hills around Boston); (b) the functional pattern of the city, particularly downtown; and (c) the structure of the freeway system itself.

Boston's present image has many weaknesses which this road may help to eliminate. The location of water is confusing. The Charles River lacks continuity with the harbor, which itself is seldom seen. Almost the whole south side of downtown, an area of extensive railroad yards and industry, fades in the image; in fact the entire area surrounding the peninsula suffers from the inner ring "grayness" that character- izes almost every American city. There are also potentialities in the image. From the air or on a map, Boston possesses a formal clarity that is not apparent on the ground. Large open spaces that surround the peninsula might provide excellent viewing points were they accessible, and Boston's internally distinctive districts could help to create a highly differentiated and comprehensible image were their character exposed to the view from the road.

To overcome the difficulty of orienting on a circular route, three major inter- sections, leading to North, South and West radials are proposed. These intersections, acting as strong forms in confused areas of the city, become apexes of a triangle, the sides of which are visually associated with that part of the city being traversed. They are called the Riverway, Centerway, and Crossing, and each possesses a central climax. The Riverway parallels the Charles River at some distance, then, at the center, kinks inward and downward to the water's edge with cross-views to Cambridge and the State House, before continuing its parallel course beside the river. The Centerway is direc- ted towards the financial and shopping district with a central outward curve around the financial district allowing views across the harbor to the airport. This curve is articu- lated at both ends by descent into areas of visible activity--to the north, Boston's Italian market; to the south, through the Dover Street tunnel, where a tunnel restaurant is proposed. The Crossing passes quietly through residential areas except for a curving stretch through Fenway Park with Kenmore Square and the baseball stadium to the north- west, and a new symphony hall square to the southeast.

The whole route contains a simple basic rhythm of intersection-climax-inter- section which is overlaid by another rhythm marked by the two major downtown destina- tions: (a) the financial district, government center, and retail shopping around the Hub, and (b) the new Prudential-John Hancock complex around Copley Square. These major goals are picked out for viewing with regular frequency and alternating emphasis along the route, so that eastern travelers relate to the Hub, western travelers relate to the Prudential-John Hancock group. Within these major rhythms lie those of secondary goals, particularly those of outlying centers (South Boston, Mission Hill, Cambridge, Somerville, Charlestown and Logan Airport) that provide rhythms of inside to outside viewing. (These and other aspects of the design, such as location of advertising, parking garages, the night scene, and road detail are described more extensively in the monograph. The drawings illustrated employ a notation system, which was developed

Fig. V-1
Inner Belt Expressway, Boston; Structure of Road

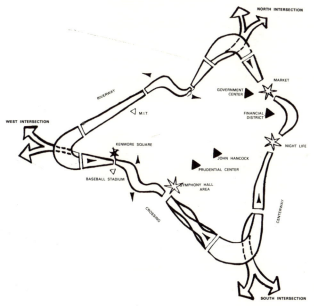

Fig. V-2
Clockwise Route

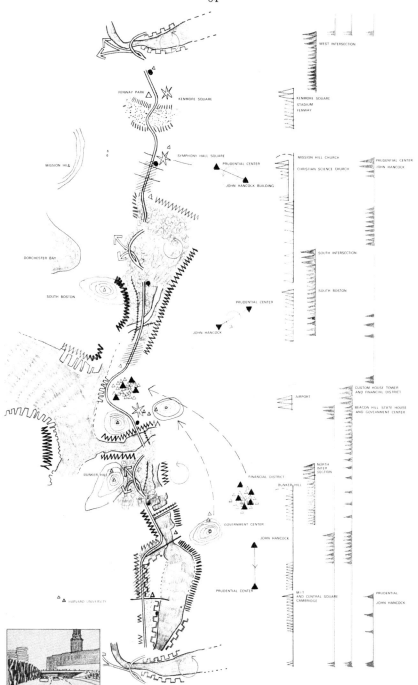

Fig. V-3
Orientation Diagram

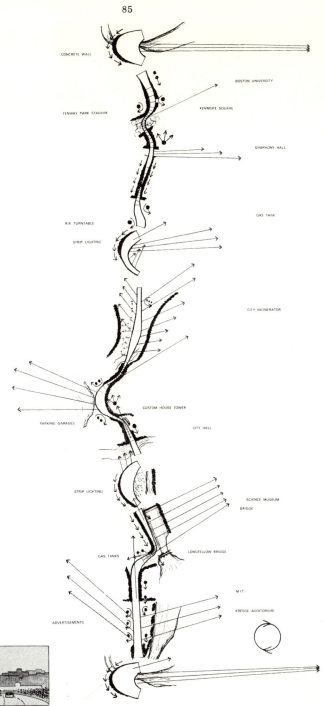

CONCRETE WALL

BOSTON UNIVERSITY

FENWAY PARK STADIUM

KENMORE SQUARE

SYMPHONY HALL

GAS TANK

R.R. TURNTABLE

STRIP LIGHTING

CITY INCINERATOR

CUSTOM HOUSE TOWER

PARKING GARAGES

CITY HALL

STRIP LIGHTING

SCIENCE MUSEUM

BRIDGE

GAS TANKS

LONGFELLOW BRIDGE

M.I.T.

KRESGE AUDITORIUM

ADVERTISEMENTS

Fig. V-4
Space, Motion, and View Diagram

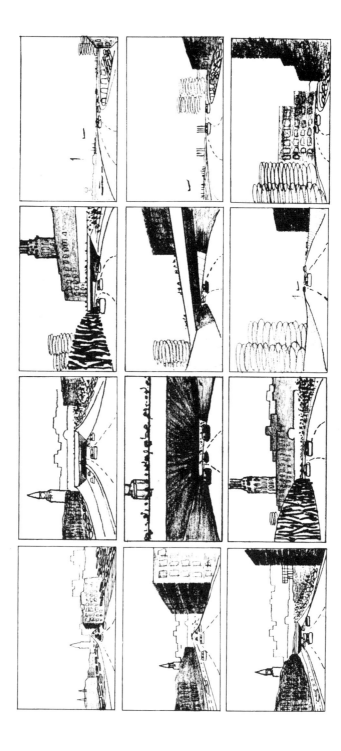

87

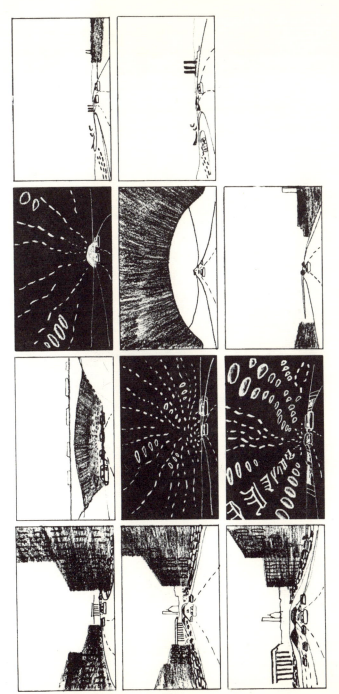

Fig. V-5
North-south Sequence on Centerway

to describe existing routes.)

    This whole study was motivated by the promise of the new world of vision inherent in the speed of movement, and by a desire to find a visual means for pulling together large urban areas. The crucial test will come in applying these ideas to actual design problems, and in evaluating the results obtained. Not only would one learn much of technical interest from a serious attempt in this direction, but a road built for vision in motion would be a concrete example of what the highway experience could be, an example far more powerful and evocative than any number of paper projects. Might it be possible to construct such a road as a national experiment?